Praise for *SuperCompetent*

"The Productivity Pro, Laura Stack, should be known as the Productivity Doctor. This book is like a medical clinic for those seeking to become more productive. I know it has helped me, but more importantly, the remedies offered by Laura have benefited the people I coach in my professional life. These people keep asking, 'Jeff, how do you know how to solve my productivity problems?' My secret weapon . . . this book."

> —Jeff Bettinger, Director Talent Development,
> Fluor Corporation

"This content-rich book is a must read for even those who thought they were productive. Laura Stack delivers specific strategies that will definitely boost your performance and productivity. Her relevant ideas will take you beyond good to SuperCompetent. This book will change how you think about yourself, your time, your use of technology, and your time with others."

> —Lisa Ford, Author of a number one selling training series,
> How to Give Exceptional Customer Service

"Ask executives which employees are most valuable to the organization, and they will almost invariably respond, 'The people whom I can point to a problem or opportunity and know that they will get the job done every single time.' These are the SuperCompetent people—who are in control of their work—not the other way around. Laura Stack teaches us how to stress less, get much more done, and have more fun while doing it. Reading this book will make a positive impact in your work and your life. Fabulous!"

> —Joe Calloway, Author,
> *Becoming a Category of One*

"Laura is a master at her craft and offers innovative ideas on how to squeeze the most out of our daily lives. Productivity is more than just staying busy; it's about achieving success and significance in everything you do. She unlocks the secrets to how we can all do more, be more, and have more each and every day."

> —Dr. Nido Qubein, President, High Point University;
> Chairman, Great Harvest Bread Co.

"Laura Stack knows how to get things done and in short order! Her latest book offers a great work-life-mind balance, which is the key to going from good to great on a personal basis. Read this book and soar."

> —Tim Sanders, Author,
> *Love Is the Killer App: How to Win Business
> and Influence Friends*

"HEY YOU! That's right, you, the person wondering if a book about being SuperCompetent is worth the investment or has any relevance to your life, career, or company. Haven't you heard? Simply being competent is for wannabes. The *heroes* actively manage their performance and productivity to achieve the results they want and need. Isn't that you . . . or at least the you that you want to be? *SuperCompetent* is that rare book that combines ideas you can implement immediately with thoughtful truths to keep you focused on what is really important. So what are you waiting for? Buy this book. Study and apply its lessons. And, give yourself an edge in your career and your life."

—Randy G. Pennington, Author,
Results Rule! Build a Culture That
Blows the Competition Away

"Every CEO should make this required reading for every employee. After 20 years of turning around the results of companies, I only wish I had this on my recommended reading list for clients earlier. Uncommon sense that will turn any organization into a Thank-God-It's-Monday Results Rule workplace!"

—Roxanne Emmerich, CEO,
The Emmerich Group, Inc.;
Author, *Thank God It's Monday!*

"Become more aerodynamic. That's what Laura Stack helps her reader to do with her tremendously practical book *SuperCompetent*. Consider the racing industry. In all of its various forms—cars, bikes, humans, horses—the principle of aerodynamics rules. Some of the smallest design changes can elevate performance monumentally. In my work with high-performing, high-potential leaders, I have found time and again that increasing effectiveness is almost singularly hinged upon decreasing interference. Simple? Perhaps. Easy? Not so much. Effective? Without a doubt. Using Laura's Six Keys, a leader can identify, diagnose, and understand specific sources of interference. Using the numerous practical tips Laura provides with each of those Six Keys, a leader can then work ruthlessly to reduce each source to perform at his or her productive best."

—Catherine Stewart, SPHR,
High-Potential Program Developer and Manager

SUPER
COMPETENT

Also by Laura Stack

Leave the Office Earlier: How to Do More in Less Time and Feel Great About It (2004)

Find More Time: How to Get Things Done at Home, Organize Your Life, and Feel Great About It (2006)

The Exhaustion Cure: Up Your Energy from Low to Go in 21 Days (2008)

SUPER COMPETENT

The Six Keys to Perform at Your Productive Best

Laura Stack

WILEY

John Wiley & Sons, Inc.

Published by John Wiley & Sons, Inc., Hoboken, New Jersey.
Published simultaneously in Canada.

For general information on our other products and services or for technical support, please contact our Customer Care Department within the United States at (800) 762-2974, outside the United States at (317) 572-3993 or fax (317) 572-4002.

Wiley also publishes its books in a variety of electronic formats. Some content that appears in print may not be available in electronic books. For more information about Wiley products, visit our web site at www.wiley.com.

Library of Congress Cataloging-in-Publication Data:
Stack, Laura.
  SuperCompetent : the six keys to perform at your productive best / Laura Stack.
    p. cm.
  ISBN 978-0-470-59915-0 (cloth)
  ISBN 978-0-470-87579-7 (ebk)
  ISBN 978-0-470-87581-0 (ebk)
  ISBN 978-0-470-87582-7 (ebk)
  1. Employees—Attitudes. 2. Self-management (Psychology) 3. Labor productivity—Psychological aspects. 4. Performance. 5. Success—Psychological aspects. I. Title.
  HF5548.8.S687 2010
  650.1—dc22   2010027045

Printed in the United States of America

10 9 8 7 6 5 4 3 2 1

To my SuperCompetent son,

Johnny Stack,

who always gives his best and goes over and above.

Your creativity and intelligence inspire me.

CONTENTS

ACKNOWLEDGMENTS

One can't be SuperCompetent without the help of a lot of people. My thanks go to my husband, John Stack, for his love and unfailing support. I couldn't ask for a better life and business partner. To my children Meagan, Johnny, and James: you are the inspiration for all I do. I'm grateful for your understanding as I spend countless hours in front of the computer and for your prodding to get me away from the computer.

My life is made easier by my amazing mother-in-law, Eileen Stack, who blesses me with the gift of time, helping me and our family in countless ways. My personal assistant and office manager, Becca Fletcher, is the PROductivity PROtégé and my right-hand woman. They both go over and above the call of duty to keep life running smoothly, and I wouldn't be able to do what I do without you both.

The National Speakers Association (NSA), of which I will be national president in 2011–2012, has provided me with a wealth of resources and a fellowship of speaking colleagues, many of whom have become close friends (and wrote endorsements for this book). Through you I have found an extended family.

My thanks go to Matt Holt, publisher, John Wiley & Sons, Inc., for believing in me and bringing me on board. My appreciation goes to my editor, Dan Ambrosio, whose insights always improve my work. Thanks for partnering with me to create a great manuscript.

My literary agent and friend, Robert Shepard, stands firmly by my side on our fourth book together. Thank you for your continued tutelage. I rest easy under the umbrella of your wisdom, which allows me to focus on writing and know all else is covered.

I am grateful to my angel mentor Dianna Booher, CSP, CPAE, for her love, patience, and guidance. Blessed is the person who is suddenly faced with a question or dilemma and can pick up the phone and get an answer. Your presence gives my life peace.

In addition, my gratitude goes to the many thousands of seminar participants I've met over the years, for sharing your success stories with me and validating these concepts. I am humbled by the gift of your time and attention and privileged to be able to help you in some small way. My thanks also goes to my corporate clients, who recognize the significance of this material in helping high potentials reach their goals and your companies succeed. Thank you for your confidence and partnership.

To my best friend, Darla Sanborn (and her husband Mark Sanborn, CSP, CPAE—who wrote the foreword to this book), for reminding me to play, breathe, walk, smile, love, laugh, and have fun. I thank God for the gift of you both in my life.

Most importantly, I thank the Lord Jesus Christ, for blessing me with the above people and for showering upon me the many gifts in my life.

FOREWORD

I wonder how many little boys or girls wanted to be Superman or Superwoman.

Maybe you put on a cape and ran through the house pretending you were flying. I don't recall doing that myself, but I did want to be a super hero (the Green Hornet was my idol).

What makes us want to be super *anything*?

Most people want to excel. We want to be better than average, above normal, and certifiably great at something. (One poll shows 90 percent of people think they are in the top 10 percent of performers. If you can't be exceptional, at least believe you're exceptional.)

By the time you're old enough to buy and read nonfiction books, you're probably off the superhero track. You are, however, a reader looking for ideas—ideas that will make you better as a person and possibly *super at something.*

I don't know your specific aspirations, but I commend you if you're honest enough to admit you are pursuing a superlative way of living and doing business. You are among those who want to be more than competent. Perhaps you've not thought of it this way, but you are aiming to be *super* competent, or as Laura coined the single word: *SuperCompetent.*

Abraham Lincoln famously said, "Whatever you are, be a good one." I'd like to think he was suggesting you and I ought to be SuperCompetent.

The question is: How to do it?

The answer is in this book by Laura Stack, the Productivity Pro®.

I've known Laura for years, both professionally and personally. I respect her work. She is an expert in how to get more done in less time. I also respect her personally, because she only preaches what she practices. My wife Darla and I call her the Energizer Bunny. I don't know of anybody who is able to squeeze more accomplishment into less time than Laura.

In other words, Laura is an expert and credible guide for you in how to become SuperCompetent.

However, no matter how many good ideas Laura shares, they won't do you any good unless you consistently and correctly apply them. You'll need compelling reasons to keep you on your course.

So consider: Why might you want to be SuperCompetent? The easy answer is that now is a great time to be SuperCompetent. Unemployment has reached new highs at the time of this writing. People are out of work and opportunities seem scarce. Being SuperCompetent is a good hedge against finding yourself un-employed or at an advantage over other candidates should you be looking for a new job.

There are no guarantees in life and no magic formulas, but when it comes to employability and success, being Super-Competent stacks the odds in your favor. Even SuperCompetent people can lose their jobs for reasons beyond their control, but in most organizations, the SuperCompetent have a far higher survival rate and longevity.

Of course job assurance and success aren't the only or necessar-ily the main reasons to aspire to be SuperCompetent. Being exceedingly competent—being *good* at what you do—is some-thing you should aspire to for its own sake. The game of life is short—we are told—so play hard. Doesn't it make sense that we also work hard? Shouldn't we make the most of our professional and personal opportunities and thus be maximum contributors to the overall good in the world?

Once you have the motivation to be super at what you do, you then need the methods.

Competency is learned. No baby is born competent. The baby learns the skills it needs to be competent at living. Likewise, the skills of competency are learned. In this book, Laura Stack shows you exactly what those skills are. She provides you a detailed map and list of suggestions and tactics for becoming a superlative performer and maximum producer, no matter how you make a living. You will have to invest the time to read and learn what she suggests, but you'll find the application of her suggestions straight-forward and simple.

You'll be pleasantly surprised to learn just how easy it is to go from being simply competent to *SuperCompetent*.

It's too late to become a superhero. But it is never too late to become SuperCompetent.

—Mark Sanborn
President, Sanborn & Associates, Inc.
An idea studio for leadership development

INTRODUCTION

My husband John and I have three children: Meagan, 15; Johnny, 10; and James, 8. Lately, we've been trying to teach James the importance of competition and hard work. We've tried to stress to him—with the prices of college tuition, food, gas (just about everything) skyrocketing—that schools and employers will only select and keep the best and hardest workers. So you have to do your part and work hard at school to learn. Easy enough, right?

Well, apparently he'd overheard John and me talking about this book and had gotten a little confused. As I was packing to leave for the airport one evening he said, "Mommy, I'm sorry I haven't been doing my chores and working as hard as I should. I can do better!" I said, "My goodness honey, what a grown up thing to say! That sounds wonderful to me," as I kissed the top of his head. He started to walk out of the room when he turned and quickly added, "Mommy, if I work harder, will you and Daddy not get mad at me?"

I said, "What in heaven's name are you talking about, honey?!"

"Well," he said, "Daddy said you were going to talk to some people about being good so you don't get fired. And I don't want to be the one who has to go!" After I explained I was talking about businesses and not families and reassured him with hugs and kisses, John and I had a good chuckle over it.

I am unusually excited about this book, because what I have to share with you today may indeed save your job *and* help you achieve your greatest potential.

I've been counseling CEOs, managers, professionals, and entrepreneurs since 1992, and I have to tell you it has been a long time since I've seen C-suite executives straining under the kinds of stresses we're seeing right now. I know I don't have to tell you about it; you know firsthand. The pressure is peaking at all-time highs. It seems everything that should be going up is going down, and everything that should be going down is going up. Hiring freezes, budget cuts, productivity quotas, globalization's heavy footsteps hot on your heels . . . it all points in a single direction:

> Success will come to those who can accomplish more in less time and consistently perform at their productive best. The people who achieve their fullest potential are not *simply* competent; they're *Super*Competent.

After all, competence is simply expected and the minimum standard to stay in the game nowadays. You want to be one of the High Potentials identified by your organization as someone positioned to move up. Are you ready?

Consider this: If you gave notice you were leaving the organization, would leadership fight to keep you? If this doesn't describe you, does it apply to someone with whom you work? Why do some people succeed at every challenge they undertake? Are they superhuman? No, they're not perfect; however, they are skilled and capable enough to master almost any task. Are they natural leaders? No again. Competence isn't the same as leadership; in fact, in my opinion, it's something much greater. We've all seen people in positions of leadership who fell short the moment they were faced with unfamiliar conditions. So, are the SuperCompetent exceptionally brilliant? Again, no! You can be a raving genius and yet not be nearly as capable as the person seated in the next cubicle.

> A dictionary defines *competence* as "having suitable or sufficient skill, knowledge, or experience for some purpose; properly qualified; adequate but not exceptional."

Blah. Doesn't that sound a bit . . . boring? Although it's good and necessary to be competent, it's no longer enough to be *only* competent. After all, you probably wouldn't be impressed by someone who is simply "a competent professional." Simply competent people don't stand out in the current environment, where the difference between merely having ability and being exceptional may be the difference between keeping your job and losing it. SuperCompetent people take it to another level: They possess a consistent, all-encompassing ability to be good at everything they do, no matter how general or specific. Scientists actually apply this same principle to the study of what they call competent and SuperCompetent cells. Competence is the ability of a cell to take up DNA; SuperCompetent cells do it far more efficiently.

I've written *SuperCompetent* for two primary groups of people:

1. Those who are *already* SuperCompetent. These people are generally seen as High Potentials in their organization and have been identified in Leadership Development Programs or formal succession planning as someone to watch. This book will help them achieve peak performance and work at their productive best. Because they are typically Type-A personalities who tend to work incredibly hard, they often put in long hours. Organizations need to retain these individuals and help them accomplish more in less time so they can better balance work and life.

2. Those professionals who want to *become* SuperCompetent and fill in the blanks on their skills. These people are perhaps competent in their current situation, but know they could be SuperCompetent if they received the right coaching. This book will help them learn to *think* like a SuperCompetent, so they can grow and eventually be seen as a High Potential in their organization. Fortunately, being SuperCompetent in life isn't a matter of DNA. Anyone can master the six keys to becoming SuperCompetent.

Your job reading this book is to learn all you can to reach your full potential; my job writing this book is to inspire you to grow and give you the skills to succeed.

Each chapter concludes with a summary and worksheets to use in book clubs or Leadership Development Programs. You'll also receive a web site address to obtain a bonus MP3, the SuperCompetent key assessment questions, a summary, and the action-planning worksheet in Microsoft Word format. To start a book club, visit www.theproductivitypro.com/SCBookClub to purchase discussion guides.

Consider a woman I met recently at an event where I was the keynote speaker. She sat at my luncheon table and regaled me with stories of her eight-month-old baby. She admitted that at 40 years old, she was probably a less-energetic mother than she would have been at 20, and yet she said she wouldn't change a thing. She explained she'd waited to have a baby because she had a successful career in the financial services industry and later in pharmaceutical sales. She had spent years criss-crossing the country to visit her clients. Her baby's arrival prompted her to take a job in the travel industry where she could handle corporate travel accounts from home. I instantly knew she would succeed at that, too; I had a pretty good idea she'd already turned out to be a SuperMom. In fact, I told this woman—named Caroline—that I believed she could succeed at anything she set her mind to. Although she was flattered, that wasn't my intention in telling her.

As a corporate consultant for the last 18 years, I can identify the performer I would hire in any position. I can tell when a person would do a fine job, even without much experience. How? All these professionals have mastered the six universal traits Caroline clearly possessed: the keys to becoming Super-Competent. If you want to achieve success in any area of life and across any area of work, you'll need to master them too. Luckily for your memory skills, they all begin with the letter *A*—for A+ performance, of course! (Okay, it's a little hokey, but hey, it's *memorable*.)

SuperCompetent people are better in the following areas than everyone else:

KEY 1: ACTIVITY SuperCompetent people are driven by intense focus on priorities and have a clear sense of direction.

Value determines priority; priority determines goals; and goals determine activities.

KEY 2: AVAILABILITY SuperCompetent people control their schedules, so they can make time for important activities. They know they can't be available to everyone every day, so they learn how to control their time and protect it.

KEY 3: ATTENTION SuperCompetent people are masters of focus and concentration. They develop the ability to pay attention to the task at hand and tune out distractions that aren't related to their work.

KEY 4: ACCESSIBILITY SuperCompetent people are well organized. They have systems in place to find what they want when they want it and can quickly locate the information needed to support their activities.

KEY 5: ACCOUNTABILITY SuperCompetent people possess self-discipline and self-control. They eliminate time wasters, strive for constant improvement, and don't blame other people when things go wrong.

KEY 6: ATTITUDE SuperCompetent people get the requisite skills and training when they lack ability. They have the motivation, drive, and can-do positivity to make things happen. They're proactive, decisive, and fast.

These principles are fundamental to the study of productivity and are evergreen, regardless of the technologies and changes in the workplace. In a nutshell:

You'll always have to:
1. Determine what you should be working on.
2. Make time for it.
3. Focus on those tasks.
4. Organize the information needed to complete it.
5. Be responsible for your results.
6. Never give up.

These traits are interconnected, so I'll dissect each and describe how to attain each in the following sections of this book. The good news, as I stated before, is that SuperCompetence isn't a genetic quality; rather, it's something you can learn. Transforming yourself into a SuperCompetent isn't about mantras, but mind-sets. Looking at your actions is an important part of understanding your capabilities, but it's just one part of understanding how to unlock your potential. The most important part is transforming the way you *think*.

Your mind has a tremendous capacity to change your life; the way you think determines your next actions. Because you can choose your mind-set, you can also choose to change it, which is what SuperCompetents do to make themselves the best they can be. In this book, I'll show you how to do what they've done, working on each of the Six Keys to transform the way you think.

This book contrasts the zero thinking of the simply competent with the hero thinking of the SuperCompetent professional. It describes how each thinks when faced with similar situations. When learning how to be SuperCompetent, you'll consider how you need to think to achieve the best results. Often, you'll have to dispense with your old mind-set and adopt a new one—maybe even faking it a bit until this new way of thinking becomes second nature. By repeatedly, purposefully acting in a different manner, over time, you'll change your mind-set right down to its core. Old thinking will evaporate, altered thinking will materialize, and new, SuperCompetent behavior will follow.

So, what *is* the mind-set of the SuperCompetent person, and what if you don't have it yet? Placing yourself in a new frame of mind requires stepping back, soul-searching, rethinking priorities, possibly defeating old personal roadblocks, and developing entirely new thought processes you can apply in all sorts of situations. This is what will add up to the fully fleshed out, newly SuperCompetent mind-set. You can use this book to help yourself, your company, and even those around you—not just momentarily—but all the time.

Implicit in this is the idea that even people who don't intuitively possess the Six Keys can learn them. My goal is for this book to help any decently capable but perfectly ordinary person achieve SuperCompetence without becoming a superhero. In fact, we're all endowed with an amazing capacity for mastery. It's a shame some of us realize this potential while many more of us fall short. The traits that so often cause people to squander their competence actually aren't traits at all—just bad learning or thought processes that can be unlearned once they know how.

Bottom line: We can *all* learn to be SuperCompetent!

THE SUPERCOMPETENT ASSESSMENT

How close are you to being SuperCompetent already? Take the following quiz, and you'll figure out exactly what you need to work on. You don't have to read this book from beginning to end; you can jump right to the section you need most and start your program there.

NOTE TO READERS: Leaders and HR managers may want to use this book to identify traits of potential Super-Competents within the organization or as a coaching aid for High Potentials.

Scoring
1 = to no extent
2 = to a little extent
3 = to some extent
4 = to a considerable extent
5 = to a great extent

THE SUPERCOMPETENT ASSESSMENT

ACTIVITY demonstrates value and reflects importance.

1.	I know exactly why I work hard and what I'm trying to achieve.	1	2	3	4	5
2.	I know what to do, when to do it, and why.	1	2	3	4	5
3.	I create systems to perform tasks more efficiently so that I can leave the office on time.	1	2	3	4	5
4.	I regularly rest and recharge my batteries in order to be productive and creative when I return to work.	1	2	3	4	5
5.	I accomplish the day's most profitable and valuable tasks.	1	2	3	4	5

SUBTOTAL YOUR ANSWERS 1–5:

THE SUPERCOMPETENT ASSESSMENT

AVAILABILITY is driven by Activity.

6.	I refuse requests when appropriate and know how to say no graciously.	1	2	3	4	5
7.	I set appropriate boundaries and protect my time from others.	1	2	3	4	5
8.	I push tasks down to the lowest level of responsibility, trusting others to do their jobs.	1	2	3	4	5
9.	I schedule my day realistically according to my key activities.	1	2	3	4	5
10.	I weigh the results of attending each meeting against the alternative results I could produce instead.	1	2	3	4	5

SUBTOTAL YOUR ANSWERS 6–10:

THE SUPERCOMPETENT ASSESSMENT

ATTENTION *is the capacity to concentrate.*

11.	I do not live in my e-mail inbox; I remain focused on my work.	1	2	3	4	5
12.	I leave distractions for my downtime.	1	2	3	4	5
13.	I know I can only focus on a few items at a time, so I limit my multitasking in order to maximize my productivity.	1	2	3	4	5
14.	I don't allow socializing—whether online or in real life—to overwhelm my productivity.	1	2	3	4	5
15.	I know technology and my handhelds are tools to help me be more productive—no addiction here.	1	2	3	4	5

SUBTOTAL YOUR ANSWERS 11–15:

THE SUPERCOMPETENT ASSESSMENT

ACCESSIBILITY *is the ability to organize the inputs and outputs in your life.*

16.	I've created the perfect time-management system for my personality, job environment, and work situation.	1	2	3	4	5
17.	I know exactly where I'm supposed to be and exactly what I should be working on at all times.	1	2	3	4	5
18.	My e-mail is organized, and my inbox is regularly emptied.	1	2	3	4	5
19.	I keep careful track of my contacts and my communications with them; I can tell you what was said in a meeting a year ago.	1	2	3	4	5
20.	I don't waste time while traveling; I'm efficient and get a lot accomplished.	1	2	3	4	5

SUBTOTAL YOUR ANSWERS 16–20:

THE SUPERCOMPETENT ASSESSMENT

ACCOUNTABILITY recognizes the buck stops here.

21.	I take personal responsibility for handling my time and productivity; I never lay the blame on anyone else.	1	2	3	4	5
22.	When I see an unusually lengthy and inefficient process, I do what I can to make it easier for everyone.	1	2	3	4	5
23.	Rather than waste even small amounts of time, I get right to work.	1	2	3	4	5
24.	When I have all the information I need to proceed, I make decisions quickly.	1	2	3	4	5
25.	I understand that the difference between being busy and being productive is results.	1	2	3	4	5

SUBTOTAL YOUR ANSWERS 21–25:

THE SUPERCOMPETENT ASSESSMENT

ATTITUDE is your motivation, drive, and proactiveness.

26.	I keep an eye on my stress level and realize that it is a mistake to ignore my emotional health.	1	2	3	4	5
27.	Even when a task is monumental, I keep working at it until I whittle it down to size.	1	2	3	4	5
28.	I am creative and open to change; I always seek better solutions.	1	2	3	4	5
29.	I adjust my approach with difficult work and time styles; I work well with all different personalities.	1	2	3	4	5
30.	I am a positive person, even in negative circumstances.	1	2	3	4	5

SUBTOTAL YOUR ANSWERS 26–30:

SCORING

COPY YOUR SUBTOTALS:

KEY	SUBTOTAL
1. ACTIVITY 1–5	_____
2. AVAILABILITY 6–10	_____
3. ATTENTION 11–15	_____
4. ACCESSIBILITY 16–20	_____
5. ACCOUNTABILITY 21–25	_____
6. ATTITUDE 26–30	_____
GRAND TOTAL = SUPERCOMPETENT (SC) SCORE:	_____

To make your score meaningful, visit www.TheProductivityPro.com/SCscoring and enter your data.

Based on an initial sample of 250 survey responses, if you have a score of —

123–150: *You're already SuperCompetent.* Congratulations! All you need to do is fine-tune a bit. Keep it up and help others raise their SuperCompetence whenever you can.

112–122: *You need a few tweaks here and there.* You're on the right track! Strive to improve wherever you made less than a 5 on your assessment. Give yourself credit for what you do well and acknowledge where you need to improve.

88–111: *Average.* You're middle of the road, which is a bit boring. You're not the worst employee ever; you're not exceptional, either. Who wants to be average? Work on kicking it up a notch!

67–87: *Major overhaul required.* SuperCompetence isn't out of your grasp, but you'll need to get serious if you want to reach it. Select one item on this list every two to three weeks and work on systematically improving your competence level.

30–66: *Danger!* Your competence level is flatlining; you need a jumpstart, stat! Both your health and your job depend upon it, so start working hard *right now.*

Get additional resources, audios, videos, and more at www.SuperCompetentBook.com.

PART 1

SuperCompetent Key 1: Activity

SuperCompetent people are driven by an intense focus on their priorities.

ACTIVITY demonstrates value and reflects importance.

This key gives you a sense of direction throughout the day.

We've all been there. It's the end of the day. Your schedule was jam-packed. You crossed 27 things off of your to-do list. Yet you still have a nagging feeling that the whole day slipped by before you got the chance to accomplish anything of much value.

Being busy is one thing. Being productive is something else. On the surface, it can be hard to tell the difference, which is why it's often easy and tempting to fall into the "busy" trap. As much as we supposedly revere productivity in today's workplace, busy is a false badge of honor. Stacks of papers covering a desk, a frazzled dash to the coffee machine, and all those blue streaks of Outlook (un)availability (wow, you're important!). It's easy to show how busy you are, but productivity is something much more personal—and much more significant.

At the end of the day, productivity is the only thing that matters. Everyone knows that a person who works an eight-hour day can be more productive than someone who works twelve. You need to be sure your time is not only accounted for, but has real value. Nobody cares how many things you crossed off your list or how busy you were last week if key projects are falling through the cracks. Only results matter. So think about how you can get the most value out of every day.

CHAPTER 1

What's It All About, Alfie?

| SUPERCOMPETENT Hero Thinking: | I know exactly why I work hard and what I'm trying to achieve. |
| SIMPLY COMPETENT Zero Thinking: | I'm working hard trying to accomplish "it," but I don't know what "it" is. |

Michael Cane starred in the classic 1966 film *Alfie,* where he played a handsome, British womanizer who lives a very hedonistic lifestyle. The line, "What's it all about, Alfie?" is a highly poignant moment in the film, when Alfie pauses on a bridge overlooking the River Thames in London and reflects on his life. He realizes that despite all of his activities in life, he has achieved very little. He asks himself, "What have I got, really? Some money in my pocket? Some decent clothes? A fancy car at my disposal. And I'm single. Unattached. Free as a bird. My life is my own." Then, he pauses and says, "But I don't have peace of mind. And if you don't have that, you've got nothing. So, what's the answer, that's what I keep asking myself. What's it all about?"

Like Alfie, you occasionally need to stop and reflect upon your life and whether you are making the most out of it. Perhaps, like Alfie, your days are just spent passing time or drifting along. Do you know what you're aiming for in life? You may work so hard and are so busy that you have lost track of your dreams.

You can't be productive if you don't know what you're working toward, which is why the word *empowerment* is a popular buzzword in business circles. People who know what they're working for are more likely to buy into the productivity goals of their teammates, superiors, and everyone else in the organization. If you're self-employed, you might say, "I *am* the organization. Of course I know what I'm working hard for."

But is that true? Do you have a set goal in mind, or are you just ambling along, marking time? It is admittedly more likely that a sole proprietor is going to be more aware, in general, of his or her ultimate goals than a worker bee in a big corporation. You need to get clear quickly. You might want to be a successful full-time freelance writer or the best plumber in town, but you can work so hard on the day-to-day operations of your business that you lose track of your dreams.

In this chapter, I'm going to offer a few simple suggestions to help you get back onto your goal-oriented track.

Know What Makes You Tick

I started my speaking and training business in 1992 by teaching professionals and organizations how to achieve their goals through increased productivity. Random House published my first book, *Leave the Office Earlier*, in 2004. Many things have changed in my life and in business during the 18 years I've been a professional speaker. One thing that has not changed is my passion for personal productivity and peak performance. It was then, and continues to be, my professional mission in life: to build high-performance productivity cultures in organizations by creating Maximum Results in Minimum Time® with greater profits.

We all have a special purpose in life and a particular calling. People sometimes ask me why I'm so fanatical about helping people energize their lives and hone their time-management skills. There's no doubt that helping people boost their productivity and maximize their profits brings me professional satisfaction. However, the truth is, as a wife and a mother of three young children, I do what I do because I know how special and fleeting time truly is. At the end of your life, you won't regret having attended one less meeting or taken one less call from a client, but you *will* miss the memories you never took time to make with your family. The best thing you can spend on the people you love is *time*, which is why productivity is so important to me.

Why is productivity important to you? There's no one-size-fits-all answer. My "why" is likely different than yours, and one of the keys to productivity is *finding* your "why." For most people, an external reason like "My boss expects more of me" isn't always the most motivating factor. You must get to the heart of *why* you do what you do to be truly motivated. Is the need to be more productive exciting to you, or does it exhaust you just to think about it? If the latter is true for you, perhaps you haven't gotten clear on why being productive is important.

It all comes down to your personal goals and what you want the picture of your life to look like. Sure, you may need to be more productive at work to make your boss happy or boost company revenues. But how can you turn it around and make it important to you personally? If you're motivated by extra time with your family, then make your priority getting things done at work so you can enjoy your weekend free from work stress. If making more money is what drives you, give yourself achievable daily or even hourly goals of what you need to accomplish to make those extra sales. Figure out what truly motivates you, then try to relate each task to a goal you have set for yourself—not one that someone else has set for you. For example, if you're in sales, your organization sets a sales goal for you. While you should absolutely do your best to achieve it, make it about *you* at the same time. How many sales are required to earn the commissions you need for a family vacation, buy the fabulous pair of shoes you want, or get the country-club golf membership?

It's only human to be motivated by what feels good, so use that. What makes you feel good? Each task you accomplish—however difficult or dull—gets you closer to that great feeling. If you can figure out how productivity relates to your personal goals, then the quest for it becomes exciting, rather than overwhelming.

Luke, It's Your Destiny

Just like Luke Skywalker, you have to acknowledge and accept that you're the only person responsible for your life. Stop blaming others for the outcomes of situations that you actually control. It's vital to own your own destiny and set your own priorities. What ideas are worthy of your time? What *must* get done? When you outline your priorities, your goals become clearer. Then you can limit your workload by mastering what's important and tossing what isn't.

Stay Focused on Your Mission

I was at a wedding reception recently and had a profound conversation with an old family friend. I asked about his flight, knowing he'd run into a few snafus along the way. He smiled and said, "The flight was fine. I'm delighted to be here." I replied, "I heard about the rain and the flight delay. That must have been frustrating." I proceeded to regale him with stories of other friends who got stuck in Denver over Christmas during a recent blizzard.

His wise response: "Oh, it didn't bother me. *I had a mission, not an agenda.*" He shared that he had adopted this motto as a rule for living. Having a mission keeps him from getting lost in the minutia. By not trying to live by other people's agendas, he's not focused on ego, but rather on his mission. As he was talking, I could just picture him waiting in Zenlike tranquility for the long-overdue airplane to arrive, while his flying companions were standing in line, flailing and fuming at the ground crew.

It was exactly what I needed to hear: "I have a mission, not an agenda." So often when launching a new endeavor, we get caught up in the agenda of the day—or worse—someone *else's* agenda for us. We lose sight of our purpose. My friend's words served as an important reminder to all leaders to not get distracted by the details, but rather stay the course and focus on the mission—*your* mission! Circumstances must never trump contentment.

How Do You *Know* When You're Being Productive?

Do you stay productive while you're working toward your mission, or are you just busy? Watch out for this one, because it's an easy trap to fall into. Everybody likes to look busy. Some workers make a career out of it, while actually accomplishing very little in an average day. People zoom around the office, guzzling coffee and stomping back and forth to the copier; they scatter paper across every inch of their desks and furiously clack away at their keyboards while they talk on the phone. Busy, busy, busy!

But motion isn't momentum; velocity doesn't equate to value; activity doesn't equal accomplishment; and rushing doesn't mean results. We all know what it's like to have a busy day but still feel like we accomplished little.

So be realistic. Set and achieve attainable goals. Everyday interruptions and the inevitable fires will still sidetrack you, but you'll be able to douse them. Having a plan will help you get back on track.

Do You Plan Your Day?

This means more than simply keeping track of your meetings and jotting down deadlines. Planning your time is about organizing your projects and long-term goals and managing your priorities. If you never look beyond your daily to-do list, it's easy to spend your day reacting to low-priority tasks without even realizing it. Sure, you'll probably go to each of your meetings and cross off a few items on your list; however, this is no guarantee that you're maximizing your productivity and making sure your daily activities are contributing toward your long-term objectives.

Take a few minutes each day to invest in longer-term planning. Double-check to make sure every meeting you attend advances your goals. Knock out your top priorities first and then chunk away at future projects.

It's easy to decide to spend time on a low-priority task in the heat of the moment. Let's face it: Fun, easy, low-stress tasks are tempting because they allow you to cross an item off of your list right away; we *all* know how good that feels. But resist this temptation. If you do the most unattractive but highest value task on your list first, you'll build momentum for the rest of your day.

Do You Have Written Goals?

And are you moving toward them? Your biggest professional and personal goals become your obsession and the object of your focus. They represent your career ambitions, your dreams for your family, or those for yourself. If somebody asked you about them, you'd probably agree your big goals in life are your highest priorities. So why is it is so easy to neglect them?

Our next promotion, our relationships with our kids, our physical fitness—whatever matters most—often gets pushed to the back burner. It's too easy for unimportant work to steal family time, for office frustrations to make you lose sight of career ambitions, or for exercise to be the entry on the list that always becomes secondary.

Grab a piece of paper and write down your goals for the next month, six months, and year. Then post this list where you can see it on a regular basis—near your computer monitor at work or on your bathroom mirror at home—so that it can act as a constant reminder of your true priorities. Make sure your goals are clearly written and post them with pride.

Productivity is about reaching high-value goals in every area of your life, often in the shortest amount of time (but not always—such as spending time with loved ones). It isn't about striking lines across a to-do list. Time-management techniques, electronic/paper planners, and other productivity aides are just *tools*, and they're only as useful as what they help you accomplish. Make sure your biggest, most important goals create the context for the other things you do throughout the days, weeks, and months.

Grab Your Dreams by the Horns and Get Going!

I wanted to use the first chapter to shake you up and remind you of why you're trying so hard in the first place. You have to know what makes you tick. What propels you toward your dreams and goals in the first place? Are you striving as hard as you should? Or have you gotten bogged down in day-to-day minutiae? This is a common problem with people who'd like to be more productive.

Your next step is to take responsibility for your life. If you're stuck in a particular situation, don't blame others for it. Step back and take a look at what you can change. Control your destiny and determine whether some of the things you're doing are keeping you from achieving your goals and dreams—and get rid of them if you can. Once you've done that, focus on your goals in laserlike fashion.

CHAPTER 2

Why the Heck Are We Doing It *This* Way?!?

SUPERCOMPETENT Hero Thinking:	I know what to do, when to do it, and why.
SIMPLY COMPETENT Zero Thinking:	I work on tasks in the order they come across my desk.

A re you comfortable in your work environment? Do you take initiative and do what needs to be done when it needs to be done? Do you examine your processes and take steps to make them more streamlined and efficient?

Or do you just do *what* people tell you, *when* they tell you, in the same old way you always have?

This type of thinking won't cut it today. People willing to put in the effort to structure their time and processes effectively are going to out-compete you, and you might find yourself scrambling to make a living—or going under.

So what do you need to do to turn things around? Here are a few ideas to consider.

Be a Must-Have Person

You have to be indispensable. Economic necessity can force budget cuts and cost containment that might otherwise be unnecessary.

One way to prepare yourself for this reality is to be very clear about how you and your team contribute to the company's revenue. Sometimes this is easy. If you work in sales, for example, the correlation between what you do every day and the company's financial success might be straightforward: My group sells our most profitable product, which makes the company money.

However, that correlation isn't always so obvious. If you operate in a support role, like Human Resources, you may want to start by looking at your various responsibilities and deciding which among them has the greatest influence on the company's bottom line, either by driving revenue somehow or controlling expenses. Perhaps you contribute to developing talent within the company, which clearly has an impact on the organization's overall success. Employee development always seems to be one of the first things to go during down economic times, but this isn't the time to reduce training if you'd like to get more work from fewer people. Or maybe you're managing clerical or administrative functions that would be more expensive to secure elsewhere.

You have to know how your actions boost your company's profitability. Your other contributions might be valuable, but in difficult economic times, corporate leadership often becomes much more focused on dollars and cents.

Where am I going with this? It's simple: If it isn't obvious how your role benefits the company, be prepared to explain how it does. And if you can't explain why certain aspects of what you do are valuable, then it's time to stop doing them.

At the end of the day, productivity is about more than getting things done. It's about getting the *right* things done efficiently.

Revisit Your Objectives

When was the last time you reviewed your job description? As time passes, it's easy to drift away from your formal responsibilities and objectives. This can be bad if you're doing work you weren't hired to do, but it can be *extremely* bad when it comes time for a performance review. Be aware of what's expected of you and know the criterion on which you're being evaluated. Sometimes you'll need to realign the priorities that have been driving your schedule, and occasionally, you and your boss might agree that your job description should be adjusted based on your evolving role in the company.

Know Your Job Inside and Out

This one should be a no-brainer, but you'd be amazed at how often our responsibilities can slowly evolve without our realizing it. Incremental changes in how employees or departments do business can add up over time, leaving groups of people who work hard but aren't contributing to business objectives as effectively as they once did. For example, in an effort to provide an exceptional level of service, you might find yourself doing work below your pay grade. Maybe you end up doing a large portion of the administrative work associated with a project that needs your input.

Consider the value of your time. Make sure the things that occupy your time are worthy of your talent and expertise and hold your staff to the same standard. With any project, you should be able to look at the time spent, multiply that by the pay rate of the ones doing the work, and still feel your resources were well spent. If a $40,000/year employee is stuffing a bunch of envelopes (even just one time) or a six-figure manager is assembling an important presentation page-by-page, those activities become awfully expensive.

These examples might seem outrageous, but they happen all the time. Never make the mistake of treating your time like it's free. Time and other resources are limited, and we need to regard them that way.

As your company and department are being asked to do more with less, now is the time to take stock of the work you're doing. Although roles and responsibilities frequently change, job descriptions do not. As a result, we end up drifting away from core priorities and toward doing work that, although challenging, doesn't meet the organization's immediate needs. Therefore, now might be a good time to step back and ask that all-important question: "Why am I (or we) doing this?" If you can't answer that—or if the answer doesn't make sense—it's time to make a change.

Practice Purposeful Abandonment

I once worked with a training manager whose administrative assistant was generating training reports for the various divisions. The task took about four hours each month. However, she wasn't sure how her internal customer used the reports. She called each contact and said, "We generate this report for you, and we're happy to continue to do that, but we just wanted to check out its importance with you. How do you use it? Is it valuable? Can we skinny it down a bit? Can we stop sending it altogether?" It turned out the recipients looked at a particular graph on page five—and that was it. She changed it to a quarterly report, with the graph and an executive summary, and the customer was perfectly happy.

When you keep the communication open with your customers—both internal and external—you discover exactly where value lies. If you put a note in the e-mail text of the next report you send out that says, "Call me if you want to continue receiving this report," how many calls would you get? Would anyone notice if you stopped doing it? This can be a humbling exercise and can deflate your ego if you discover no one needs what you do. However, it will allow you to focus on what you could be doing to add greater value and abandon the things that diminish it.

Specify the Appropriate Detail Level

I once worked with the president of an automotive parts manufacturing company, who called an analyst in finance to get a figure to put into his PowerPoint presentation. The president assumed the analyst would spend 15 minutes on it and be able to quickly ballpark a number. Turns out the employee spent 10 hours coming up with an exact number to the seventh decimal place. All that the president was seeking was a high-level guess: "Is it 5 million or 50 million?" Who was at fault for the miscommunication? They both were. The president should have said, "I'm looking for this type of number, and I'm thinking it'll just take you 15 minutes or so to ballpark it, plus or minus a few million dollars. Does that sound reasonable?" Then the employee could tell him what it would actually take to create that figure he wanted, and the president could decide if it was worth it for that particular speech. The

employee could have also said, "The information you're requesting will require me to do X, Y, and Z, which will most likely take
(this) many hours. Is that what you want?"

Reevaluate Your Productivity Habits

The end of the year is a prime opportunity to look over how
things have been going and look forward to see how they could
improve. But you don't have to wait until January for that fresh
start we all want. Make the most of every day!

What are your daily frustrations and biggest obstacles to your
personal and professional productivity? For sanity's sake, you might
have chosen to pick your battles and unwittingly plunked yourself
deep into productivity quicksand over the years. Maybe you've re-
signed yourself to the fact that staff meetings are always a waste of
time and have stopped trying to improve them. Or maybe it's as
simple as giving up on making it out the door with a decent break-
fast in your belly.

Well, no more! Take next month by storm and reexamine the
way you get things done. Who knows? You just might make some
headway on an issue you thought was a lost cause years ago. Here
are some ideas to consider:

1. _Challenge the status quo._ Does the task or project necessarily have
   to be done like this? Many people—including yourself—don't
   like change, but you don't have to remain stuck in an unproductive rut. All too often, we resign ourselves to deciding a
   result is "good enough" and accept a mediocre outcome.
2. _Is there a recurring meeting at work that makes everyone groan and
   hasn't been worth the hour it eats up for as long as you can remember?_
   Maybe it's time to reconsider how that time is spent. If you
   have any say in how the meeting is run, perhaps your
   group's resolution should be to get it back on target. Or
   maybe it's simply time to get rid of the meeting altogether
   and give everyone involved a little extra time in their day—
   a precious thing, indeed.
3. _You know the time drains:_ Status reports no one reads, inefficient
   paperwork, and time-tracking techniques that never see the

light of day. Things like this point to an underlying problem: No one steps up to say "why are we doing this?" So take a risk and speak up. Especially when it comes to projects that are large or critical, people can get uneasy about changing a process. After all, there's a lot at stake, and the old way has never failed before. But the result can be a clunky, overly complicated process that is more difficult and stressful than it needs to be. Make some waves! It may be a little stressful the first time around, but you might work your way toward a new system that will save tons of time and future aggravation. Don't be the one who suffers in silence out of fear of rocking the boat.

4. *When you're reevaluating a process that seems complicated, consider working* backward *to find a better solution.* When you begin at Step One, it's too easy to fall back into familiar patterns and miss the point of what you're trying to do. Instead, begin at the end and look back. Start with the final result you want to achieve and build a new process from there. You'll be much more likely to discover steps that could be either tweaked or axed altogether. Get your team together—armed with pads of sticky notes and a bare wall—and challenge yourselves to eliminate several steps.

5. *Structure is your friend.* You may have a job that is so process-heavy you forget that having a defined procedure in place is, under the best of circumstances, a good thing. So make sure you find a way to put a system in place when you're dealing with a recurring task or an assignment. Structure is especially important if you're working in a group; you need to make sure everyone is on the same page in terms of who's responsible for what and when. A checklist can be a great asset here. Simply note everything that needs to be accomplished and who's responsible for doing it. If your process stalls, you'll have no problem figuring out where the problem lies.

6. *Measure!* If you go on a New Year's diet, you're going to step on the scale at some point for an objective look at how things are going. Without a no-nonsense measurement, it's difficult to gauge your success or failure. It's hard—nearly impossible, in fact—to improve what you can't measure. How would you know if you've succeeded? This is particularly true when it comes to tweaking or creating processes. Keep track of the

changes you make and evaluate how they have improved productivity. Did you make the process faster? Does it involve fewer people? Did the quality of the work improve? Ask yourself these questions whenever you question a longstanding process. If you keep these questions in mind before you make any changes at all, it can help guide your decision making.

Rattle the Cage!

Go for it! Don't be afraid to tackle the issues that stand between you and your personal or professional productivity. Work is usually done a specific way for a reason, but the reason may not always be obvious. It may turn out to be something people do because they've always done it that way. Well, business processes usually aren't like that old-time religion—just because it was good enough for your father doesn't mean it is good enough for you. Things change, especially when it comes to technology. After all, we're not still driving buggies and using slide rules.

So mix it up. Take a look at how you do things and see if you can't prune out the things that make you less productive. Be willing to practice purposeful abandonment, trim out unnecessary detail, and measure whether or not the processes you're using are as effective as you think they are. You can go back to the old way if the new one doesn't work out.

CHAPTER 3

Greater Living Through Technology

SUPERCOMPETENT Hero Thinking:	I create systems to perform tasks more efficiently, so I can leave the office on time.
SIMPLY COMPETENT Zero Thinking:	I'm working 80 hours a week already, so if I can work more quickly, I can pack in something else.

Decades ago, a series of labor organizers fought hard—some even losing their lives in the process—to ensure Americans only had to work 8-hour days and 40-hour weeks. Don't look now, but those gains have been eroding steadily for the past two decades. We work harder and longer now than we have in years. The High Potentials among us would laugh at the whole idea of working a mere 40-hour week, but even so, they too tend to work much harder than they have to and probably should. Whatever happened to time off?

Schlimmbesserung, Anyone?

For decades, productivity experts have been gazing at their charts and graphs and trying to envision what would come next—without much success. They imagined by the twenty-first century, we'd have so many electronic devices doing our work, we wouldn't know what to do with ourselves. A robot would sweep the floor, do the dishes, and perform calculations while we slept. In the morning, as self-running kitchen machines made your toast, they'd have completed a perfect glossy report and fixed your flying car's engine. And with supercharged productivity in the workplace, we could spend most of our day at the spa or the theater.

In 1966, the *Wall Street Journal* wrote, "the highly productive employee of 2000 will work a week that his 1966 counterpart would envy . . . It will be only 31 hours long." Other experts said we'd be working 3 hours a day. Arthur Pack, the author of 1932's *The Challenge of Leisure,* predicted a *2-hour* workday. And after an exhausting adult life of working 2-hour days, we'd be set to retire around age 40.

Are *you* working a 10-hour workweek? I didn't think so.

It turns out the biggest energy crisis in twenty-first-century life is how to find the power to complete everything. Many of us future folk feel as though we're working 22-hour days, and we'll never be able to retire. We feel as though *we* are the robots, programmed for unceasing routine tasks. This is a scary thought when you realize the word *robot* comes from the Czech word for slave, *robotnik.* (Playwright Karel Čapek coined the term for a 1921 play.)

So what happened? (And while we're at it, where's my flying car? I was looking forward to whooshing around on a jet pack by the year 2000, too.) The forecasters were right about one thing—we now have laborsaving technology that relieves us of many routine tasks. Yeah, right!

My roots are German, and my grandfather used to have a word for this kind of technology—*Schlimmbesserung* (shlim-BESSER-ung). It loosely means "a so-called improvement that actually makes things worse." Instead of using all our extra leisure time to take in an opera or go roller skating, Americans see these technological tools as a way to *get more done.* We take on more tasks and raise our expectations of what we should accomplish in a shorter period of time.

This isn't anything new, by the way. Before the invention of the vacuum cleaner, your grandmother or great-grandmother had to take all the rugs out of the house and beat them with a stick to get the dirt out—a *huge* job. So you'd think a vacuum cleaner would give the homemaker much more free time, right? It didn't. Why? Because in the old days you might take your rug out for a good shake once a year during spring cleaning. But once you had that vacuum, the standards of cleanliness went up, and people started vacuuming once or twice every week.

Schlimmbesserung!

Remember the prediction of the paperless office? We were supposed to be working in those by now. But the thousands of computers we own have one thing in common: They're all hooked up to printers. When e-mail was first introduced in an office, the number of printed documents went *up* by 40 percent. So much for the paperless office! Instead of doing away with paper, we're being called on to produce shiny brochures and reports and pie charts—simply because we can.

That means you have to spend hours designing documents and checking them and then fighting with an expensive copier because you *know* it has a feature that allows you to bind and staple it automatically—a task that would take you a good hour on your own. Then someone has to file and organize all those reports, and e-mails, and brochures, and receipts, and other random papers. Oh right—that someone would be you.

Schlimmbesserung!

Call waiting . . . fax machines . . . e-mail . . . pagers . . . smart phones . . . iPhones . . . technology continues to provide us with more ways to communicate with each other, only succeeding in making us feel more scattered and disjointed. Meanwhile, the number of things worth talking about remains the same. A *real* improvement would be if Microsoft or Apple came up with a way to spell check your grocery list so you could read your own handwriting, do a keyword search of your house so you could find the documents you lost on your desk, and run a "defrag" on your life.

Where Does the Time Go?

When people feel fatigued and overextended as a result, they tend to blame it on *time*. "Oh, if I only had enough time . . ." *A lack of time is not the problem.* This is a bit like blaming the Internet because your boyfriend sent you a nasty e-mail. There are 24 hours in each day; there always have been, and unless something drastic changes, there always will be.

I know, of course, you often *feel* as though there's less time than there used to be. Recent research tells us the number of people who say they have less free time than they did five years ago is twice as high as the number of people who say they have more free time. (Makes you wonder how big a grant they got to study that issue.) But here's the thing: Even with all these Schlimmbesserungs, you actually *do* have more free time than people had in the past—quite a bit more.

In John P. Robinson and Geoffrey Godbey's 1997 book *Time for Life*, the authors describe how Americans have almost five hours more free time per week than they did in the 1960s. In fact, we average about 40 hours of free time per week. (*Free time,* by the way, means time away from work, meals, housekeeping, child care, and sleep.) We've gained almost *one hour per day* since 1965. Yet most people in the study felt they have *less* free time than people in the past. They also estimated about 16 hours a week of free time, much less than they actually have. As people feel more stressed, they tend to exaggerate the length of time they spent at work, so they use *lack of time* as shorthand for feeling stressed or exhausted. We're willing to accept *being busy* much more readily than *being tired* or *overwhelmed.* The truth is we are lousy with time!

We feel so overwhelmed because we're every bit as bad at predicting our own futures as the experts are at predicting the future of the human race. Famed Dilbert cartoon creator Scott Adams put it this way: "There are many methods for predicting the future. For example, you can read horoscopes, tea leaves, tarot cards, or crystal balls. Collectively, these methods are known as nutty methods. Or you can put well-researched facts into sophisticated computer models, more commonly referred to as a complete waste of time." So much for predicting the future.

Two North Carolina researchers recently published their findings on the science of procrastination. They surveyed 900 volunteers and discovered that people idealize the future and expect they'll be less busy then. For some reason, we all seem to be time and energy optimists. We picture our future work as if nothing else will be going on in our lives. "Sure, I have energy to work full time and go to school full time and have four children." But we forget the rest of our lives will still be there too. "Oh gee, I still have to walk my dog and take out the trash. My wife still wants attention. I didn't expect my mother to go into the hospital. Who knew there would be a wedding that month? Did I just volunteer to chair a committee?"

It's not actually the *amount* of time that gets us, but the number of things we have to keep track of—and the amount of energy those tasks require. It isn't so bad to mistake fatigue for overwork or laziness, but when you can't identify the problem, you have a much harder time coming up with the correct solution.

So you buy a new productivity suite for your computer and stay up until 3:00 AM to get it running; now you're exhausted over the next two days and don't have the energy to learn it. That type of productivity is counterproductive. This is where you must be crystal clear about your Activities and the most valuable priorities you must accomplish.

Take Back Your Time

You know, as much as I'd like to have one of those flying cars the futurists have been promising, I'll bet when they do come around, they'll be more trouble than they're worth. After all, look what vacuum cleaners, photocopiers, cell phones, and electric dish-washers have done for us. We work harder and longer than ever *because we can*. Say it with me: "Schlimmbesserung!"

Even things that are supposed to help us relax, like TV, end up stealing our time, turning us into zombies who don't even realize we have the leisure time we do—because we've wasted it. Americans have more downtime than ever before; we just have to be willing to use it. There's no need to wear yourself into a frazzle and then fritter away your free time in front of a screen or working. You'll end up a pleasureless drone—a theme that feeds directly into the next chapter.

CHAPTER 4

All Work and No Play Makes Jack a Dull . . . Something

| SUPERCOMPETENT Hero Thinking: | I regularly rest and recharge my batteries, so I can be productive and creative when I return to work. |
| SIMPLY COMPETENT Zero Thinking: | I can't take a vacation, because I'll be so behind when I return! |

What if I said your productivity would improve by taking a full vacation, laughing more, and having more sex? You like me better already, I can tell. Well, it's true. Working nonstop without breaks is counterproductive, as is focusing on work to the exclusion of family, friends, and fun.

Some people claim to be so swamped they don't have time for a break—not for vacation, not for a social life, not for anything. I am *severely* unimpressed by people who brag about the long hours they put in each week. All this tells me is they're not managing their time well. You have to figure out how to get the results your job requires in as little time as possible, leave the office on time (or at least earlier than you are now), and get home to a life. If you're working too many hours, perhaps you're not delegating properly . . . or you haven't hired enough people . . . or you don't trust your assistant . . . or you haven't learned to use your e-mail program correctly . . . or you're a paranoid control freak.

Now, let me be clear: It's perfectly normal to occasionally work a 75-hour week when you have an important project deadline. Great. *But then things should go back to normal.* Alan Robbins, who founded the Plastic Lumber Company, summed up this view when he said, "My social life is low at this point. I call it the SSC rule for entrepreneurs—sex, sleep, and cash flow. One out of three is all you can expect when you're starting a company."

Take a Break Before *You* Break

Your problem isn't a lack of hours in the day; it's a lack of energy to accomplish tasks. The symptoms of laziness and lack of energy are remarkably similar. Boring, monotonous, unbroken work and staring at a computer all day without a break saps your energy, but taking care of yourself *increases* your energy. Laughter, time out in the sun, and intimate time with your partner all boost the immune system, provide cardiovascular benefits, and just make you feel good. They're worth taking the time for. Your productivity will improve, and your personal life won't hurt either.

Guilt Starts with a *G* for Garbage

We all need to stop and smell the roses on a regular basis, but for some reason, we seem to feel guilty about taking time off. This can be particularly true of mothers who work outside the home. I promise you no one's head is going to burst into flames if you take a hot bath. Your life won't fall apart if you sit on the porch swing and enjoy the spring air. It might, however, fall apart if you don't!

Time is valuable. You have to savor it and make time for the things that electrify your life and ignite your joy. That time recharges your battery, so when you're on task, you can be productive. Give yourself the gift of time.

You can't ignore your need for rest any more than a driver can forego the oil for his car engine. For a short time, the car might move along, but overheating will soon lead to sputtering. It's the same with your need for leisure. Neglect it, and the consequences will hit you sooner than you think.

V–A–C–A–T–I–O–N (in the Summer Sun)

We need "recreation" to re-create, restore, and renew. This is something other nations seem to realize. Outside the United States, mandatory vacation time ranges from 10 days in Canada and Japan, to 20 days in the Netherlands and the UK, 24 days in Germany, and 25 in Sweden and France. How much vacation is required in the United States? *None.* In fact, every year, American workers give up billions in unused vacation time.

Rest isn't the enemy. Down time is not wasted time. Another name for downtime, as a matter of fact, is *your life.* We're not "human doings" after all—we're human beings. No wonder we feel tired when we're scrimping on our own lives!

And while we're talking about vacation, it's not fair if you only take working vacations. A real vacation doesn't involve your laptop by the pool, a BlackBerry while standing in line at an amusement park, or a side trip to meet with a client. It involves a brightly colored drink with a paper umbrella in it. Some people are so used to living on the hamster wheel that they don't know how to be on vacation. Even if you need your iPhone and can't leave it back at the office, you don't know how to flip off the urgency switch in your head. These people are easy to spot. They're on a beach in Puerto Rico, highlighted by the glow of a dazzling sunset—and they're vibrating. They're yelling at the operator of a shuttle boat because they *need* to get back to the hotel *right now* because they have a *very important tour bus* to catch. There are sights to see! If you find yourself with gritted teeth saying, "I'm here to have fun, dammit!" or if your itinerary allows no more than five minutes to gaze at each historic sight, then it's time to rethink your vacation strategy. I recommend something with a hammock.

If you're used to operating in high gear all the time, this may be harder than you think—and *exactly* why you need to take your full vacation.

Quit Banging Your Head Against the Wall

We have a lot of fears when it comes to taking time off. We're afraid we'll lose our focus or lose our place. The notion that great things are achieved by single-minded focus is widespread but baseless. Evidence tells the story. For example, how do you explain the embarrassing fact that the greatest inventions of history normally come from individuals who never had a formal education in the fields in which they achieve their breakthroughs? Albert Einstein wasn't a physicist, and Louis Pasteur wasn't a medical doctor. A musician invented Kodachrome film. A sculptor created the ballpoint pen. A veterinarian came up with the pneumatic tire. An undertaker invented automatic telephones. Two bicycle mechanics fashioned the first airplane. And a 16-year-old high school student invented the television.

As Anonymous once said, "We don't know who first discovered water, but we can be sure it wasn't a fish."

Rest, for Goodness Sake!

Creativity and productivity are not the results of constant, grinding work. Even the most productive among us needs to take the time to recharge our batteries. Don't overdo it and become a slacker, but *do* take the time you need for R&R.

CHAPTER 5

My To-Do List Has 117 Things on It!

SUPERCOMPETENT Hero Thinking:	I accomplish the day's most profitable and valuable tasks.
SIMPLY COMPETENT Zero Thinking:	I'm going to try to get as many things checked off my list as possible; I work to get things done.

Do you start *and* end the day overwhelmed, wondering if you've accomplished anything? If so, you probably haven't. Too often, people respond to brushfires as they occur. They feel as though they worked hard, but in reality it's like the tale of Shakespeare's idiot—full of sound and fury, signifying nothing. And even when they're working from a to-do list, most people use the quantity-over-quality rule: They feel more accomplished when they can chop 20 things off their list in a day—never mind the fact that the one thing left over is 100 times more important than everything else put together.

Does this sound like you? If so, here are a few things you can try to make your daily efforts more worthwhile.

Eliminate To-Do List Anxiety

To-do lists aren't all bad. My biggest problem with them is that each item seems to take on the same level of importance. If you look at a list of 50 things, it's overwhelming. "Oh my goodness, I have 50 things to do! I need to finish this report by Friday, book my hotel for the business trip, send an e-mail to my client, learn Russian, and wash the dog!" Well, washing the dog would take ten minutes, as will writing that e-mail. But each ends up as just another item on the list of "things to do." As the list gets longer, you get more and more stressed. "How can I possibly complete 50 things (or 200)? I can't. I won't even start. Is *American Idol* on television tonight?"

The good news is that your list of 200 things is easier to tackle than you think.

You can start by getting the smallest key tasks (like e-mailing your client) out of the way so they won't sit there bugging you. Then, clean up your workspace. Get rid of the mess, the clutter, anything that might draw your focus. Then prioritize. What's important? Don't start by doing the fun stuff. Start with the *valuable* activities. Where do you need to focus?

You'll probably need to admit there's a lot of stuff on the list you're never going to do. "Okay, I can cross 'learn Russian' off the list." Few things sap more energy than the ongoing mental drain that comes from hanging on to a project you will never get to or complete. Priorities change, so be willing to call a spade a spade and move on.

Take a tip from Nancy Reagan and learn to just say no. You can accomplish just about anything you want, but you can't accomplish *everything* you want. Your energy is finite. Every time you say yes to something, you have to say no to something else, or risk doing it all—*badly*. Feeling like you're not doing well at anything you're doing is emotionally draining. So try to preserve your energy for the things that will move you toward your goals.

This Task Is Dying a Slow Death on My To-Do List

Why do some items on your to-do list never get done? Reasons range from the classic (too many interruptions) to the matter-of-fact (I don't feel like doing it). Following are the top 10 issues at the heart of the problem and some guidance on how to deal with them.

1. *You haven't made the necessary decisions.* Your to-do list should be full of clear, actionable ideas, that is, things you can actually do. If you set a vague goal—like "Have a sale"—then you've still got a lot of thinking to do before you can hit the ground running and make real progress. Take a minute to figure out what you need to accomplish: What kind of sale? When will it take place? What will it promote? Once the task is more fleshed out, you're more likely to make progress on it.

2. *You haven't talked to the people involved.* Are you worried you lack the necessary support to make your idea happen? If you need buy-in, go get it. Your first step should probably be to pick up the phone or schedule a meeting. Even if you don't get the answers you want, you'll at least know where you stand. From there, you can move forward, adjust your strategy, or simply move on. Wherever the idea ends up, at least it isn't festering on your list.

3. *You haven't done your homework.* Perhaps you know you need to schedule a webinar series but haven't gotten around to researching which platforms are available. Figuring out mundane logistics is likely keeping you from making an important decision. Carve out some time to do the legwork or, better yet, delegate part of the task to someone else. Once you have a better idea of your options, you can focus on the real issue at hand.

4. *You're ignoring your internal clock.* We spend so much time focused on schedules and deadlines we often forget to pay attention to our body's natural rhythms. Yes, your Outlook calendar might say that a block of work will fit perfectly on Wednesday afternoon, but if that places your big task in the middle of a low-energy period of your day, you don't stand a chance. Keep your daily energy level in mind as you plan your time. Start high-energy projects early in the day if that's when your concentration is at its best; if you're slow to get going in the morning and are more of a night owl, then you should wait until later on.

5. *The task is unpleasant.* The first step is admitting it! Be honest with yourself; there's probably an item on your list that you've been avoiding because it's tedious, or you'd simply rather not do it. Get tough with yourself. Make a decision right now to do the task, delegate it, or forget about it altogether. If you need to do it, stop mulling it over and get it done. If it can be delegated effectively, make arrangements with someone else. And if you're going to eliminate it completely, cross it off your list, and move on!

6. *The task is overwhelming.* Sometimes you simply don't know where to start. Is there an item on your to-do list along the lines of "Complete Huge Multifaceted Project XYZ"? No wonder you aren't making progress: the task is too big. Large or complicated projects need to be broken down into smaller chunks; otherwise, they'll always take a backseat to the more manageable things on your list. After all, would you rather spend the afternoon completing five smaller items, or barely making a dent in one? By identifying the key steps—such as "Gather project documents" and "Outline project scope"— you'll know exactly what needs to be done next, and be less likely to hesitate as you take action.

7. *You're plagued with distractions and interruptions.* Seemingly inno- cent interruptions—like checking e-mail, answering the phone, or chatting with coworkers—will eat your produc- tivity alive. Although many of these interruptions aren't necessarily your fault, managing them *is* your responsibility. Identify your time wasters and take immediate steps to cor- rect the problem. You might need to set regular times each day to check e-mail, or close your door to let coworkers know you're temporarily unavailable. Not sure where your time is going? Keep a detailed log for a few days and find out (go to www.TheProductivityPro.com under the Productivity Resources menu and look for Free Stuff for a time-log activity).

8. *You're constantly putting out fires.* Does it seem impossible to achieve any real long-term focus as you jump from one urgent, immediate priority to the next? High performers understand how important it is to make time for truly high-value activities,

even if they don't present themselves as urgent, deadline-driven issues. If you spend every day jumping from one issue to the next, you might help avert disasters, but you won't ever accomplish anything substantial. Instead, focus on the causes behind all those urgent interruptions. Do they come from lack of planning, procrastination, or a team that isn't empowered to handle simple issues on their own? Once you address the underlying problems, you'll be able to focus your time and energy where it belongs.

9. *The task requires a lot of work for little reward or recognition.* Recognition is nice, but don't live and die by it. If the task is worth doing, it's worth doing regardless of whether you'll be recognized for the contribution. If it's not worth doing (but you have to do it anyway), then just get it done—and move on to something more fulfilling. In the meantime, your paycheck is your reward.

10. *Your day is overscheduled before you even sit down in the morning.* You schedule time and bend over backward for everyone else—why don't you do the same for yourself? Make appointments with yourself and treat them with the same level of importance as you would a meeting with a client or coworker. If you know you need three hours to get something done, schedule three hours to get it done. And I mean *schedule* it. Put it on your calendar, eliminate distractions, and treat the task with the same respect you would a one-on-one meeting with a live person.

So there you have it: ten huge productivity bandits. Decide which ones best apply to you, and be relentless as you kick them to the curb and get those tasks checked off your list!

Handling Low-Priority Items

If you already know you should work on the most important things first, the next big question becomes, "What should I do with all the lower-priority items?" Here are seven questions to help you confront the rest of your list:

1. *Can someone else handle the task?* Your goal is to push the activity to the lowest pay grade possible *without* compromising the results. I used to sort my mail every evening and get it to the right people in the office. Once I relinquished a bit of my obsessive control over the process, trained my assistant on how I wanted it done, and resisted the urge to go to the mailbox, I saved about 20 minutes a day. She picks it up on her way into the office, and after several months, there hasn't been one thing that couldn't have waited until the next morning for me to see. Part of my learning here was to stop seeing my mail as a gift— like a child dying to open her Christmas presents—and realize it was simply another task demanding my time and attention.

2. *Can you simplify the process?* I give 80 to 100 presentations every year on personal productivity topics. Every client needs certain information from our company to publicize the meeting or event. Since different staff members in our office handle different areas (travel, logistics, contracts, and so on), the client would receive multiple e-mails. Instead of sending multiple attachments from multiple people, we simplified the information into a single Meeting Professionals guide: A multipage PDF file that provides all the information in one place, via one e-mail, from one person. No more confusion on whom the client should ask and who has already provided what. Any person in our office can see in real time what another just sent to a client.

3. *Can you become more efficient?* Once an engagement was underway, a client might need additional information not initially provided in the Meeting Professionals guide—such as a photo, course description, or my introduction. After sending this information piecemeal to whomever needed it, we put it on our web site after each request. Now we proactively let clients know at the time of booking where they can find anything they need with links. We have more information than anyone would probably want on the web site; if it's requested more than one time, we add it. This requires less staff time on our part, and clients can get what they need more quickly. How can *you* be proactive in providing information to people before they request it?

4. *Can you stop doing it?* Have you ever asked yourself the question, "If I didn't do this at all, would anyone notice?" What a

darn good SuperCompetent question! It's important to keep the communication open with your customer, find out what has value, and abandon what doesn't. If you are doing your work, the work of another person who was laid off, and the work of a coworker on maternity leave, something is not going to get done, period. What's it going to be? Hopefully, the low-priority items.

5. *Can you create a checklist to handle repetitive tasks quickly?* Before I leave for a trip or speaking engagement, I have to know certain things are in place: Books are shipped, ground transportation arrangements are made, workbook copies have been produced, an LCD projector will be available, and so on. So we automated the process. At the time of the booking, a checklist is placed in the central client hardcopy file; each staff person checks off tasks as they're accomplished or filed. I simply have to pull the file and scan the checklist to see what's been done and note any exceptions. This ensures each person completes all the necessary tasks prior to an engagement, and I don't have to ask or check in.

6. *Can you lower your standards?* Does it have to be done *perfectly*? Have you ever spent an hour crafting the absolutely ideal e-mail message to your internal staff, when all that was required was something quick and dirty? Invest the time when it makes sense, and be willing to be less than perfect when the outcome isn't worth the time investment. Your high standards are commendable, but if they weren't necessary for the task, they wasted a lot of time and effort.

7. *Can you use a shortcut?* Use a standard response template for information you provide repetitively to different people (such as replying to media requests for quotes, thanking people for kind feedback to a presentation, sending invoices, and so on). I used to keep standard templates in Microsoft Word and cut and paste them into Outlook, which is better than retyping them each time. But I have saved even more time by setting up the standard templates as Signatures in Microsoft Outlook and titling them by the type of response or letter. I simply create or reply to the e-mail, click Insert, Signature, and pick the name of the signature, customize a couple things like the name or date or dollar amount, and hit Send. Simple! What a great shortcut.

Taming the To-Do Tyranny

Let's face it: For most of us, to-do lists are indispensible guides to our lives, especially the daily ones we construct every evening to delineate exactly what we need to get done the next day (you do that, correct?). But it's too easy to fall into the trap of assuming everything on your list is of equal importance, which clearly isn't the case. Does ordering party favors for a friend's baby shower compare to completing a draft for a million-dollar contract? No. But it's tempting—and it is human nature—to get those little tasks done instead of jumping on the megatask, just to check a few items off your list. And yes, it's also tempting to put off the onerous yet pressing tasks. But don't! Unless you can delegate them, you've got to get them done, and putting them off doesn't serve you.

Hopefully, these examples will give you a few ideas on how to get high-priority activities done and how to deal with low-priority items on your list. Remember that productivity isn't measured by how many hours you work or how fast you work. It boils down to how much value you produce in the time spent.

SUMMARY: ACTIVITY

Productivity requires propulsion. You're never going to be productive if you sit like a lump and don't get to work. Think of all those failure-to-launch kids who seem to plague modern society. These boomerang children come back home and live in their parents' basements because they can't get a career started. Why? Well, let's leave the underlying reasons to the sociologists to ponder and simply be frank: For whatever reason, they've lost track of Key 1: There's no Activity in their work lives, so there's no real work life.

Even those of us out in the rat race every day may be sabotaging ourselves by failing to put Activity into play properly. Super-Competent people know that value does *not* equal velocity; you can be busy all day long, running from one brushfire to another, without accomplishing anything productive at all. True Activity has a purpose that gives you a sense of direction. It's all about knowing your goals and working toward them in a constructive manner. It's also about not being hidebound by the old ways of doing things if it's possible to do something more efficiently. This is critical, because nothing gets in the way of getting things done like useless dinosaur thinking.

Incidentally, just because you find a process that streamlines your overfilled schedule—whether it involves taming your to-do list by doing the hard things first, abandoning useless tasks, or learning quicker ways to do things—don't assume that means you can now fit a whole new task into the empty slot. For heaven's sake, you're not a *robotnik*, are you? Use your newfound free time to go home earlier than your usual 7:00 PM and be with your family, build a new model Ferrari, or play a round of golf—whatever having time off means to you. As long as you don't become a slacker and start playing hooky with your increased efficiency, taking time off can be one of the healthiest, most productive things you can do.

Go to www.TheProductivityPro.com/Activity to receive bonus material, the SuperCompetent Key 1 assessment questions, a summary, and the action-planning worksheet in Microsoft Word format. Get additional resources, audios, videos, and more at www.SuperCompetentBook.com.

ACTION PLANNING WORKSHEET: ACTIVITY

1. I know exactly why I work hard and what I'm trying to achieve.
   What came to mind when I read this?

   _____

   _____

   _____

   _____

   What is my action plan for improvement?

   _____

   _____

   _____

   _____

2. I know what to do, when to do it, and why.
   What came to mind when I read this?

   _____

   _____

   _____

   _____

   What is my action plan for improvement?

   _____

   _____

   _____

   _____

3. I create systems to perform tasks more efficiently, so I can leave the office on time.
   What came to mind when I read this?

   _____

   _____

   _____

   _____

What is my action plan for improvement?

_____

_____

_____

_____

4. I regularly rest and recharge my batteries, so I can be
   productive and creative when I return to work.
   What came to mind when I read this?

_____

_____

_____

_____

What is my action plan for improvement?

_____

_____

_____

_____

5. I accomplish the day's most profitable and valuable tasks.
   What came to mind when I read this?

_____

_____

_____

_____

What is my action plan for improvement?

_____

_____

_____

_____

PART 2

SuperCompetent Key 2: Availability

SuperCompetent people are masters of their own schedules.

Your AVAILABILITY is driven by your Activity.

This key acknowledges that you can't be available to everyone all the time.

This key acknowledges you can't be available to everyone all the time, so you need to protect your time to accomplish your desired activities.

You must commit to making the changes necessary to take control of your life. Just as setting valid priorities and goals is important, so is accepting your responsibility in carrying them out. If you don't determine your schedule, other people will do it for you. How many times have you attended a meeting and asked yourself, "Why am I here?"

Determine how to protect your time from everyone who wants a piece of it. Think about ways to eliminate unnecessary meetings. Learn to leverage technological productivity tools, such as GoToMeeting, videoconferencing, and services like Jott.com or dial2do.com, that can lighten your scheduling load, accelerate productivity, and streamline your schedule.

CHAPTER 6

You Want It WHEN?

SUPERCOMPETENT Hero Thinking:	I refuse requests when appropriate; I know how to say no graciously.
SIMPLY COMPETENT Zero Thinking:	I want to please everyone, so I agree to all requests.

Have you ever found yourself trying to make plans with a friend, play with the kids, or do something fun for yourself—only to find your planner so full that "maybe next month" is the best you can do? If so, you probably have that old Ado Annie syndrome: you're just a girl (or guy) who can't say no. We all want to feel like great parents, accomplished workers, and helpful members of the community. Saying, "Yes" is a good thing—in *moderation*. It's human nature to want to succeed and please others. But how much is too much?

Productivity doesn't mean filling every moment of every day with tasks that further some agenda. Prepare yourself for upcoming burnout if your schedule is so full there isn't time for family, friends, and, yes, *you*. You're good at what you do, so people will always ask for your help and your input. They want you to join another board, sew the costumes for the school play, or write the homeowner's association newsletter. Just because your calendar has a blank time slot doesn't mean you have to acquiesce to someone's request to fill it.

No Isn't a Four-Letter Word

Time management isn't about magically finding more hours in the day; it's about making the most of the ones you have. So stop hunting for spare minutes and start refusing to fill your calendar in the first place. If you keep taking things on, when are you going to get the actual work done?

You know you're going to get a call or e-mail soon saying "Will you . . . ?" So be prepared. Take a deep breath and say it: "No." That wasn't hard, was it? Okay, you don't even have to say the actual word. Get creative! Here are some alternative ways to say no without actually saying it:

1. *Negotiate.* Don't assume the deadline. One woman asked me, "I'm an admin, so I'm essentially in a customer-support role, and my job is to give people the information they request. How can I say no to them?" The answer isn't to say no but rather ask questions. Many times we assume people mean "right now" when they make requests; ask them specifically, "Do you need it today, or will Monday be okay?" Or say, "Here's a list of the things I'm working on today. Does this take precedence?" Have your manager or customer help you prioritize the order.

2. *Communicate.* Setting boundaries is a process of negotiation, so have a conversation. I received an e-mail from a woman who described her boss as "urgent." She said, "Everything absolutely, positively had to be done the day before yesterday. After giving me three urgent projects for the week, he'd race in, vibrating, with another urgent project. He had much more urgency, however, than he had memory. At first I tried to treat every project as urgent, but soon it became impossible. I learned quickly to remind Mr. Urgent of all the projects he'd given me and to ask him to prioritize them. 'I can get to this right away, but is it more important than the urgent project you gave me this morning, or the urgent project from yesterday?' Being able to prioritize gave the whole list much less intensity,

and probably saved me from an ulcer or two. Now I tell him, 'Here's a list of the things I'm working on in priority order. Where would you say this falls?'"

3. *Reduce Quality*. Determine the value of executing a task perfectly by finding out exactly what's expected of you. You might be going well above and beyond what's needed. Perhaps you're preparing an elaborate weekly status report when those who read it are only interested in the single diagram on page three. If they ignore the rest, just distribute the diagram. By getting an idea of what recipients use the report for, you might turn a 2-hour headache into a 20-minute piece of cake. Perfection has its place, but if the benefits of your work aren't worth your time, you should reconsider what you're doing for the sake of personal productivity. Ask, "What level of perfection is required here?"

4. *Streamline*. It's important to keep communication open with your customer—even if it's your boss—in order to discern what has true value. Ask if the full-color, 30-page bound report you prepare every week is essential, or if you can slim it down and still preserve what others want and need to see.

5. *Eliminate*. Do you have trouble turning down work from other areas of the company? Now is the perfect time to start fresh and rebuild your department's boundaries. Honestly explain to others that current economic realities have prompted your group to streamline daily operations by eliminating certain types of requests to build efficiency. Again, ask yourself, "If we didn't do this at all, would anybody notice?" If the answer is no, then stop doing it.

6. *Get Creative*. Perhaps you need to apply a little systems-type thinking and reconsider the flow of information. Construct a diagram of how work moves through your department. Figure out where it comes in and goes out to other departments. Interview your internal customers to find out how you can provide value through reduced services. For example, can you perform a report quarterly instead of monthly? Can you cancel the weekly project meeting and get everyone to e-mail updates instead? Can you cut down on travel if a conference call will do? One of the best ways to take stock of the situation is to survey your group, find out what gets in the way of

productivity, and genuinely find out how they would redesign things if they could.

7. *Partial Delivery*. If nothing else, try to complete a project piece-meal when you're overwhelmed: "I can get this first part done and get the rest to you by Friday." If you find you shouldn't be doing the task in the first place, then redirect it: "That request actually goes through IT; I'll make sure they know about this problem."

Break Habits, Build Systems

Every office has certain unwritten policies and procedures that exist simply because "we've always done it that way." These tradi-tions aren't good enough for SuperCompetent people. Analyze your existing business practices and find opportunities to break the bad habits that may be bogging your operation down. Consider your department: Do you and your people have a clear idea of your area's specific responsibilities? Do you have the confidence and determination to say no when someone is asking you to do work outside your scope of responsibility?

Perhaps your group took on the responsibility of coordinating quarterly meetings with senior managers over the years. It might have made sense for you to be doing the legwork then, but now that the work has become routine, is it the best use of your talent and resources?

Always question a task when an employee wonders, "Why am I doing this?" Rather than spend another day mindlessly plowing through projects that may be a waste of your time, force yourself to take a hard look at what's taking your time and why you're doing it.

What are your department's top three priorities in terms of tasks or responsibilities? Once you agree on those, evaluate how much time and energy you must dedicate to each. You might be surprised at how much time we can spend doing things that aren't even close to the top of the priority list.

It isn't always easy to say no. Fortunately, your systems can help you here, because they can give you the ammunition to fend off those inclined to slide work onto your plate where it doesn't belong. If you don't have firm policies and procedures in place to identify who should be doing what, it's much more difficult to make the case for saying no.

Refuse to Let Yourself Be Overwhelmed

It's been said that the reward for a job done well is more work—especially when the work is done competently, underbudget, and more quickly than expected. The problem is that the reward here soon runs up against the Law of Diminishing Returns. Too often, if you're good at what you do, you end up with more on your plate than you can handle. The solution is to find subtle—and sometimes not-so-subtle—ways to keep people from loading you down with too much work. I hope the strategies I've outlined in this chapter will help you accomplish the mission.

CHAPTER 7

YOU! Off My Planet!

SUPERCOMPETENT	I set appropriate boundaries and protect my
Hero Thinking:	time from others.
SIMPLY COMPETENT	I allow others to tell me where to be and
Zero Thinking:	when; other people dictate my schedule.

Interruptions account for a large portion of wasted productivity in anyone's life, whether you work in an office or at home. I'm reminded of the guy who was pulled over by a cop for speeding, who muttered, "What a jerk!" As the cop approached, his little kid in the back seat yelled out, "Here comes the jerk!"—and of course the ticket was inevitable at that point. But isn't that how we are as adults when people come into our office to interrupt us? "Here comes the jerk!" Unfortunately, we can't exactly say that at work (though you might say it in your head).

The Six Ds of Interruptions

In general, interruptions fall into six basic categories. I like mnemonics (as you can probably tell by now), so I came up with all Ds for the interruptions that waste our time—the common, frustrating things that are most likely to crop up during the day. They are Deadlines, Disruptions, Dependencies, Discrepancies, Distractions, and Drop-Ins.

1. *Deadlines.* Do you tend to be affected by deadline-driven activities? Are the boxes on your calendar bursting? Let's say you have a lot of meetings and scheduled phone calls, plus so-and-so is having a retirement party, and such-and-such is having a birthday party—and of course, you've scheduled lunch. You can't possibly get any work done with all those appointments, so here are a few ideas on handling deadlines.

   • *Break it down.* We all have deadlines, but we don't have to let them tyrannize us. One way to better handle them is to split all projects into more easily manageable portions, so you don't end up doing everything at the last moment. If you have a project due in six months—like this book, for example—don't wait until a month beforehand to start on it. Determine how much you'd need to do every week to get it done, and double it for unexpected contingencies. Then try to do some work on the project each day, so you'll finish up early and have plenty of time to polish it up.

   • *Weed 'em out.* If you have a plethora of little deadlines hanging over your head, start pruning. This isn't something you should do in all circumstances, but it has to be done when you become overburdened. For example, is the weekly staff meeting you diligently attend worthwhile or a waste? Can you cancel or put off a few of your lunch gatherings to get the occasional breather? Think about what matters to you, and then put your pruning shears to work. But don't cut out all the time you need for yourself and your family (that would be counterproductive).

   • *Pass.* You simply can't attend every birthday, retirement party, and happy hour. Suggest to your department that you celebrate everyone's business anniversaries, birthdays, and retirements at one monthly celebration.

2. *Disruptions.* Crises, unexpected events, and unforeseen tasks can land on your desk like flying saucers. Even if you planned your day, emergencies are bound to erupt. To deal with them, consider establishing a temporal contingency fund to help you cope. There's not a lot you can do about unexpected events; after all, they're unexpected, right? But there *are* ways you can mitigate their effects. For example, most businesses maintain monetary contingency funds for things they can't

plan for. It's possible to do the same with time, at least to a limited extent. For instance—consider blocking out a specific amount of time during the day or week for unexpected events. If something comes up, then you can use the time you've scheduled to keep it from blowing a big hole in your schedule. If nothing comes up, you're golden—you can go home a little earlier at the end of the day or week. As they say online these days, "Woot!"

3. *Dependencies.* These are best described as open loops and situations where you can't proceed until someone else does. For example, you might be stuck waiting for information or approval to move forward. You're bottlenecked and can't take the next step until you get input from so-and-so, who is holding things up. Instead of sitting around twiddling your thumbs, try these ideas instead.

   • *Plan ahead.* Unless you're a boss who can force the bottleneck to get you the information, documents, input, or whatever you need—or else—there's not much you can do to compel dependencies. If you can plan ahead, however, you may be able to work around these roadblocks by cutting them out of the equation, which isn't easy to accomplish in a team environment.

   • *Go over or around them.* Otherwise, there's always a possibility of going over people's heads to their bosses. You should hesitate to play that card unless you're hopelessly stalled by something like sheer incompetency or office politics. When you do play it, you'll have to deal with their resentment afterward, and they may not want to play nice.

   • *Tough it out.* Move on to another project that you can move forward while waiting for the other person(s) to get back to you. Give the owner a heads-up about the impending blown deadline due to a lack of response.

4. *Discrepancies.* These occur when work is returned to you because you or someone else didn't do it correctly, such as expense forms missing receipts or purchase-order requests without complete information. Incorrect paperwork represents rework—something that was off the plate is now back on. Let's look at a few ways to keep discrepancies from stalling you.

- *Are you a hound dog?* In a situation like this, don't assume the other person is entirely at fault. Although that may be the case, consider the following: Did you explain to them properly how you needed the paperwork done? Did you hound them to get it done faster? If the answer to the first question is no and the second is yes, then the fault lies partially with you. It's worth investing the time to explain exactly what you need—especially if there are exceptions—and to wait patiently while they do it, as long as it's done on time. Do something else while you wait; you've got plenty on your plate, right?

- *Nip it in the bud.* It's also possible the person who made the mistakes is either sloppy or incompetent. If this is the case, and you have some influence over that person, emphasize the importance of doing things right the first time. Give any necessary coaching or secure required training to increase skills. If you're the boss, one of those repercussions might be losing a job. Don't make threats but do be clear about consequences.

- *Reason with them.* If the erroneous colleague is at the same level as you on the corporate ladder—or higher—then you clearly won't have the same influence you'd have over a subordinate. However, it can't hurt to calmly and rationally explain the problem to them. If they don't improve, then try to find a way to work around them. It won't be easy, but it may be your only option.

5. *Distractions.* Is your office or cubicle right next to an elevator bank or high-traffic area where people walk constantly? Do you sit next to a coffeepot or a copy machine where people are always chatting? Or do you have a coworker who talks on a speakerphone without ever shutting the door? Even e-mail can be distracting, because it pops up all the time. So what to do?

   - *Move it.* Some of us can block out environmental distractions with ease; some of us can't. Even if you can, your ability to do so might vary from day to day, or even from hour to hour. If you're bothered by all the noise or activity, see if it's possible to move to a quieter corner of the office somewhere. Most bosses would be amenable, assuming there's room; if you're the boss, then, hey, no problem. If you work out of your home and can't deal with the TV, dogs, and kiddos, then look into renting an office and working there.

- *Talk to your coworkers.* If your neighbor thinks it's just fine to listen to his voicemail at top volume or coworkers believe it's no problem to hang out outside your office and chat loudly about their Aunt Edna's surgery, call them on it and politely ask them to stop. Most people who chat in the halls don't realize they're being annoying, so they'll probably be graceful about it and move on. Now, anyone inconsiderate enough to listen to his voicemail on speakerphone may be pugnacious enough to ignore you if you ask him to keep it down. Here's a simple solution: Have someone call and leave an embarrassing message on his voicemail. Don't be too nasty—you're in this for illustration, not for revenge—but having everyone in the office hear that his application for Nose-pickers Anonymous has been approved just might teach him a little lesson.

- *Tame the technology.* Technology doesn't have to be a Schlimmbesserung in disguise. It's there to help, not hurt you. E-mail isn't a present; you don't have to respond instantly when one pops up. Turn off your e-mail alarms and notices; in most cases, you can check only once an hour or so, and you'll be just fine. Turn off your handheld unless you absolutely need it. If you need to work for a while, turn off your landline and cell phone so you don't have to deal with those, either.

6. *Drop-ins.* Coworkers are forever stopping by, your manager is constantly popping in, and those this-will-just-take-a-minute hallway meetings keep cropping up. Most of us get unexpected visitors all the time. Some people claim they can't even go to the bathroom without someone asking them to do something or requesting an update on a project! Don't let people parachute in like this and land on you. You can choose not to accept it; here's how:

   - *Establish a no-interruption signal.* Choose a "signal" with your coworkers to cut down on interruptions. We have a retractable plastic tape we pull across the door that says, "CAUTION! Productivity Pro at work!" You can use a red cap, orange armbands, police tape, a "be back at" clock on the door, or a miniature desktop flag. It doesn't matter what the signal is, as long as everyone understands and abides by the rules of engagement. Obviously, you can't wear your red cap 100 percent of the time, or people will begin to ignore your signal.

- *Limit socializing.* On the other hand, you don't want things to get too personal. Depending on the culture of your workplace and colleagues, there may be a tendency for office relationships to stray too far from the professional and too close to the personal. People say it all the time: "I'm trying to get my work done, and all Pat wants to do is chat!" That may be true, but nine times out of ten, it takes two to tango. If you're faced with an office gossip or someone who goes on and on about his or her personal life, you've probably done something to encourage the behavior. Perhaps, just to be polite, you make it a habit of engaging people like this by listening to them talk—or even joining in. They wouldn't keep coming back if you weren't providing some social payback. Chances are if you stop showing such extreme interest, they will probably find someone else to inconvenience.

Divert Those Diversions

In *The Tempest*, Miranda cries out in wonder, "O brave new world that has such people in't!" For so many of us, Shakespeare's heavy irony here is often appropriate. Who hasn't thought, at least every once in a while, "Gosh, wouldn't it be a great world if it weren't for *all these people*?" While there's nothing wrong with being sociable—heaven knows, it's one of our great strengths as human beings—we all know there are times when human behavior, whether deliberately or not, just seems to get in the way of getting things done. Often someone is distracting in one way or another, or you have to depend upon them to get things done or to get things done *right*. Even more depressingly, there are some situations in which people seem to deliberately drag their feet.

You're there to work. You want to get things done, and you want those around you to do the same, whether they're your office peers or your direct reports. So it's up to *you* to step up to the plate and take action and reduce interruptions so you can do so. Tame the wild cards in human behavior that lead you and those around you to go off on unproductive paths instead of buckling down and getting your work done.

CHAPTER 8

Anything You Can Do, I Can Do Better

SUPERCOMPETENT Hero Thinking:	I push tasks down to the lowest level of responsibility, trusting others to do their jobs.
SIMPLY COMPETENT Zero Thinking:	I don't like to give tasks to others. I can do them better. Other people always mess things up.

Once you've figured out how to do something well, it is human nature to believe you can do it better than most people. Perhaps (and most likely) you can. But you don't have *time* to do every little thing yourself, especially low-value tasks below your pay grade. Let's assume you can train someone to do something 85 percent as well as you can. While that may not be perfect, it's pretty good. And if they're doing it, *you aren't.*

And besides, there's an outside chance that, even if you're great at something, others *can* do it better. So find ways to let them try.

Let Some Tasks Go

If you value your time—and I assume that you do—you can't spend it doing tasks that aren't valuable. Take a step back and make sure even your lowest priority tasks are worth the time and effort you invest in them. Just because they manage to creep onto your to-do list week after week doesn't mean they're a good use of time. If it's an activity you do for others, make sure they find it valuable before you spend another second on it. The last thing you want is to expend effort on projects that shuffle their way through inboxes until they're finally deleted or tucked into some bottom-less filing cabinet.

Train Someone

Of course, there are plenty of tasks you'd like to skip permanently, but that isn't always an option. Still, maybe you can call in some backup. Are you the only one capable of getting it done? If so, is there someone you could train to fill the need? Even if you need to invest some time and energy now in bringing someone up to speed, you'll thank yourself down the road. Just remember when you're delegating tasks like these, you need to relinquish your per-fectionism. Worry undermines the point and power of delegating in the first place.

Know Your Limits

You're inevitably going to let people down if you're stretched too thin to perform at your best. You don't need to make up excuses; simply be honest if you have too much on your plate. When the boss asks you if you can come in on Saturday to finish the quarterly report, reply with something like, "I have prior obligations, but I can definitely have it to you by noon on Monday." The boss doesn't need to know your obligation is a racquetball game. You might think refusing gracefully will get you in trouble or you're being rude or letting someone down. But to paraphrase the great twentieth-century American philosopher Harold Francis Callahan (otherwise known as Dirty Harry), a person's got to know their limitations.

Now, I can hear some of you thinking, "Yeah, right, you don't know my boss." Or you may be thinking, "But my company is so small there's no one to delegate to." Or maybe you own your own company, or you're materially responsible in some way for the business. You're thinking, "That could work fine if you have the kind of job where you just show up, and if you don't finish, someone else will do it—but I don't have that job."

I'm sure you *do* have a lot on your plate (who doesn't?). And it's ideal if you have the staff, coworkers, and resources to delegate some of your tasks, but not everyone has the support. Still, ask yourself this question: Will you be successful if you bite off more than you can chew? Won't your boss or your buyers or clients be happier in the long run if you achieve the best results for them?

By the way, have you ever noticed how many food metaphors there are for overwork? You bite off more than you can chew; you have too much on your plate. Imagine how you feel when you are stuffed with too much food: The after-Thanksgiving feeling when all you want to do is lie on the floor and undo your belt. "I can't believe I ate the whole thing." And how effective are you when you're in that position?

When you're honest about your limits, you're looking out for the interest of your leaders, your coworkers, and your clients. You're helping them get the best output. Nothing will win you respect more than coming through with the goods in the end.

Gasp! *You* Could Be the Problem

I can think of one thing worse than a person who does nothing: the person who tries to do everything. Say it with me: "I can't do it all." The sooner you come to terms with this troublesome fact, the better off you'll be. In pursuit of being the undisputed office superstar, you may be buried. The more you try to do everything, the less able you are to do anything.

Admittedly, the business world can be demanding, but nine times out of ten, buried office workers willingly put themselves in the situation they're in. You need to be realistic about what you're capable of doing. If you accept additional responsibilities without being able to keep up with what you've already committed, you'll be unable to devote proper attention to any one of your many duties and projects.

If you think being overextended and frazzled sounds bad, imagine reporting to someone in that situation. Being spread too thin leads to missed deadlines, poor response times, and a constant source of unnecessary stress. Do your subordinates, coworkers, and yourself a favor. Keep your priorities focused and your load realistic. You need to be able to work as hard for others as they do for you. If it takes you days to respond to a voicemail or weeks to review a proposal, you aren't setting others up for success.

Create Your Outsource Team

While you're out there sparking deals, closing accounts, and taking innovation by the horns, someone has to handle the logistical details. If you're overloaded with tasks someone else can do more cheaply, hire someone to do them.

I don't care who you are—at some point everyone confronts the need to outsource tasks. In that case, the best thing you can do as a SuperCompetent is to put people in place whom you can trust—and then trust them. Specialist web sites, like eLance.com, can be lifesavers in such a situation. I've used them for scanning jobs, graphic design, logo creation, and media work. You will always have some projects that need to be done a certain way and kept to a certain standard. Keep a close watch on these tasks and priorities to ensure they're completed properly. Consider hiring out some of the rest. You can spend up to ($x) amount, correct?

This Looks Like a Job for . . . Superman's Sidekick!

OK, it's time to let you in on the deep, dark secret of Super-Competent people: Just because you *can* do everything doesn't mean you *should*. At best, you're going to end up harried and exhausted, a blockade to productive progress, and your productivity will plummet. Worst, you may end up like those Japanese salary men who die of overwork—and there goes productivity again.

The most productive (and wealthiest) people focus on the tasks that profit them most, and either trim away everything else or hand it off to someone else. The latter is especially important. In those instances where delegation is possible, you must learn to leverage delegation as a means of achieving greater productivity. I guarantee you Superman did not sew his cape. He delegated that duty. Follow his example.

CHAPTER 9

Savvy Scheduling Secrets

SUPERCOMPETENT Hero Thinking:	I schedule my day realistically according to my key activities.
SIMPLY COMPETENT Zero Thinking:	I reorganize my day to accommodate anyone who requests my time.

Most of us are willing to accommodate other people's needs. Helping others is what makes us social beings, right? But it's possible to take this too far and wind up jerking yourself around according to other people's dictates. Then you can't get done what you need to get done—and that profits no one.

Take Control of Your Scheduling Online

Using software to maintain your schedule can be extremely effective. However, if you're not careful, it can turn into a real Schlimmbesserung for both you and everyone else involved. Try to keep the following 15 factors in mind when scheduling your day in Outlook, Lotus Notes, or a similar program.

1. *As a courtesy to your coworkers, send a meeting invitation instead of an e-mail when you'd like to connect.* Rather than e-mailing

colleagues and asking, "What's your schedule like today? Can we get together for 30 minutes?" take a minute to schedule a meeting invitation. In Microsoft Outlook, start a new appointment in your Calendar and click the "Invite Attendees" button. Find an open time during their day (assuming you've been granted access to their calendars), or select AutoPick to let Outlook find the next available date/time. Then you can simply send the meeting request. When invitees receive it, they can click Accept or suggest an alternate time, and Outlook moves the appointment to their calendars for them. This saves them time and also saves you from trying to coordinate multiple calendars manually.

2. *If someone does send an e-mail wanting to meet, convert it into an appointment.* If your colleagues don't understand the meeting feature and insist on sending e-mails for appointments, you can quickly turn an e-mail into a Calendar item. Right-click on the e-mail, select Move to Folder, and then Calendar. A new appointment window that contains your e-mail and any attachments automatically opens. You can fill in the date, time, and details, then click Save and Close. The message is moved from the Inbox into the Calendar automatically. No more dragging or manual copying and pasting!

3. *Use labels to quickly see the makeup of your schedule.* Right-click on any appointment in your calendar, select Label or Categorize (depending on your version), and then select Edit Labels. Type the updated text next to the color you wish to change. Use colors consistently with your team (travel, multiple locations, training, personal, vacation, meeting, video conference, and so forth) so you can quickly see where team members are working and what they're doing.

4. *Create a private calendar to post appointments you don't want others to see.* Although we're all used to e-mail folders, most people have never created a calendar folder, which is actually a new calendar. To create one, follow the same drill for creating an e-mail folder (right-click on the Calendar in the folder list and select New Folder). However, make sure the folder contains "Calendar Items" in the drop-down box. Give your new calendar a name such as "Kids Summer Schedule" or "Laura's Personal Calendar." I keep track of my kids' activities in

separate calendars, so their events don't muddle up my work schedule.

5. *Check your appointments as Private when you don't want others to read the text.* Yes, you can actually do this! The tiny "Private" box is located on the bottom right-hand corner of your screen when you create a new appointment (Outlook 2003) or the lock symbol (Outlook 2007). People who share your calendar will still see you're unavailable but won't be able to read the appointment text.

6. *Use the Category box (or Categorize) to indicate the project, team, or committee.* Every time you schedule an appointment or accept a meeting invitation, indicate the project to which it's related in the Category box. Use the Master Category List to add your labels by tagging each appointment with one or multiple categories. Then, under the View menu, select Arrange by, Current View, By Category. This allows you to see all the meetings—past and present—that you had with a certain group, person, project, committee, and so forth.

7. *Include travel time in a single appointment and put the actual meeting time in the subject.* If your meeting starts at 11:30, but it's going to take you 15 minutes to drive there and 15 minutes to get out of the building to your car, block out your calendar starting at 11:00 (so others can't schedule with you). Then write @11:30 in the subject line, so you know the actual meeting time.

8. *Send lengthy reading materials at least 48 hours in advance.* It's frustrating to waste time in meetings reviewing extensive information your colleague distributed a mere five minutes before. Participants don't have adequate time to digest the information and formulate questions; meanwhile, they could have reviewed those documents while waiting in the doctor's office yesterday. Don't waste everyone's time by forcing them to sit there and read together like kindergarteners; their time is much too expensive.

9. *If you're updating a meeting already scheduled, send an update to the existing appointment.* If you've already set up a meeting and invited participants, sending an e-mail about the meeting forces them to either copy and paste the additional information into the meeting or have two meeting blocks for the same

event side by side on their calendars—which in turn forces them to open two items to get complete information. If you need to add information, send out a meeting update. To contact meeting attendees with a reminder or other message, open the original meeting request, click the Actions menu, and select "New Message to Attendees."

10. *Avoid meeting-request responses.* If you're sending a meeting request to a large group and don't need or want responses, then simply uncheck the line "Request Responses" on the Actions menu in the Open New Meeting Request. To make this the default, click Tools, Options, E-mail Options, Tracking Options, and "Delete blank voting and meeting responses after processing." Or create a Rule (under Tools, Rules, and Alerts, start from a blank rule) to automatically delete message responses with certain words in the subject line.

11. *Schedule time for preparation and action.* Depending on your level of involvement in the meeting, you clearly need some time to get ready. You might begin your preparation days before if you're crafting a report or giving a presentation. When you accept a meeting, immediately go into your calendar and block off at least 15 additional minutes separately for prep time, a bio break, refreshing beverages, and transfer time. Add more as necessary for mental preparation and review. Never walk into the meeting cold. You'll also want to block out time after the meeting to review action items, activate them into your time-management system, and get organized.

12. *End meetings before the top or bottom of the hour.* If you're the one scheduling the meeting, don't use the standard Outlook settings of hour or half-hour blocks. If one meeting is from 1:00–2:00, immediately followed by another from 2:00–3:00, you will, by default, be late to your 2:00. So start and end either 15 minutes or 45 minutes after the hour to allow transition time.

13. *Display multiple Outlook windows at one time.* Perhaps you want to see your calendar while looking at an e-mail. While in your Inbox, right-click on your Calendar (either on the Folder List or the icon) and select "Open in New Window." Outlook will open your Calendar in a separate window, which you can resize and move to where it's most convenient for you, while

still being able to switch back to the Inbox. This is especially useful if you have a large monitor (or if you're lucky enough to have two).

14. *Customize your Calendar to your preferences.* Don't be satisfied with the standard calendar layouts—make your calendar your own! For example, you can automatically add holidays to your calendar by clicking Options on the Tools menu, then Calendar Options, and then Add Holidays. The weekends are also compressed by default; however, if want to show Saturday and Sunday as separate boxes, right click in the Calendar and select Other Settings. Uncheck the box that says Compress Weekend Days. While you're there, you can change the default setting for 30-minute time slots to 5-, 6-, 10-, 15-, or 60-minute slots (I use 15). If you frequently schedule with people in another time zone, avoid confusion by displaying this zone by selecting Options under the Tools menu. On the Preferences tab, click Calendar Options, Time Zone, and "Show an additional time zone" check box. Select the desired time zone and OK.

15. *Use Contacts to find meetings.* Can't find an upcoming meeting that you know you scheduled? Tired of searching your calendar manually to find it? If the appointment wasn't a meeting invitation, use the Contacts box at the bottom left of each appointment to indicate with whom you're meeting. If a meeting invitation is used, this feature is automatic and you don't need to select the names. Then, to find all upcoming meetings with a particular person, go to the Contact's address card, select the Activities tab, and in the drop-down box, select Upcoming Tasks/Appointments. (The people must be loaded in your personal Contacts list—not just your company's global address book—for this feature to work.)

Block Out Time to Work

You may actually want to schedule an appointment with yourself to *work*. To protect your time from others, schedule a Task on your Calendar. Don't put something to do on your Calendar, because if you don't get it done, you have to manually change or move it.

Use Tasks instead to track things to do that don't need to be done at a certain time. With the TaskPad view or To-Do List in the Calendar showing, click on a Task you'd like to complete. Hold the left mouse key down while you drag it to your calendar and release. An Appointment window will pop up, automatically inserting the task into the text portion of the appointment item. Fill in the time you want to work on the task on your calendar, and then change the Show Time field to Tentative, if desired. Save and close. The task will still be kept in your Task Pad or To-Do list, but now you've blocked out time on your calendar to work on it. If you don't complete it during the scheduled time block, no problem. It will still be in your Tasks the following day.

Keep Your Calendar Up to Date

Let's say that your colleague is trying to schedule a meeting with a large group, and your calendar appears open. She sends out a meeting request to the entire group, and you respond, "Oh sorry, I actually have a conflict on that day/time that wasn't on my calendar." Your colleague will respond by banging her head on the desk in frustration, asking, "Then WHY didn't you have it on your calendar?" Truly, if an organization is going to predictably use shared calendaring to coordinate meetings, you must keep yours current. It's fine to use a traditional paper method as well, but if you schedule something on your other calendar, make sure to update your electronic one at regular intervals as well.

Sorry, My Schedule Is Full Until March 2139

If your time is in demand—and what productive person's isn't these days?—then you may find your schedule packed with things you need to do from the time you get up until late in the evening. This is especially true when you're juggling a family with a career, as so many of us are (a topic I address in my book *Find More Time*).

Ironically, if you end up with *too* many things to do, you won't get a lot done. Rather than thrash around, trying to accommodate everyone, apply the tips I've outlined in this chapter to tame your schedule. Yes, it'll take a little time to set them up, but they'll work with minimal tweaking later. Not only will these tactics help make life easier for you, but some of them will even help other people better understand and appreciate when you're available and when you're not.

CHAPTER 10

Stop the Meeting Madness!

SUPERCOMPETENT Hero Thinking:	I weigh the results of attending each meeting against the alternative results I could produce instead.
SIMPLY COMPETENT Zero Thinking:	I don't have the authority to refuse meeting requests.

Meetings can devour your entire day if you let them. Have you seen the Dilbert cartoon about preliminary premeeting meetings? I was rolling on the floor in my office laughing after reading that one; it was so typical of everything I see. Does it ever feel like you're stuck in a Dilbert cartoon and can't get anything done because you're *always* in a meeting? Well, you can decide not to take it anymore! Keep the following items in mind when dealing with time-stealing meetings.

Refuse Face-to-Face Meetings When Unnecessary

Determine if you *really* need to meet in person. How many times have you attended a meeting and asked yourself, "Why am I here?" Hopefully, you've started protecting your time from every person who wants a piece of it by now. If my clients want to meet in person, I charge a consulting fee. I don't charge for telephone calls. Ninety-five percent of the time, a conference call will suffice. Extra travel time and expenses are inevitably involved when meeting in person, so avoid it unless dialogue and brainstorming are required.

Do not accept a meeting invitation if the requestor can't state in one sentence the exact reason for getting together. For example:

- To inform our department of changes in the holiday pay policy.
- To sell management on our division's plan to automate payroll processing.
- To brainstorm the best way to resolve the association's budget deficit.
- To determine realistic sales goals for each region for next year.
- To discuss the critical skills required for successful performance as a first-level supervisor.

Cancel Meetings

Meetings can be important; they allow for the exchange of ideas and play an important role in the dynamics of the workplace. But not all have the same level of value. The limited number of hours in the day forces you to pick and choose when a meeting is appropriate and when it isn't. Always think twice before calling a meeting. If you have the flexibility to choose, you should consider agreeing to attend one, too (although sometimes politics trumps choice). If you feel like meetings waste a good deal of your day, consider the following:

- Is the meeting simply to exchange information? If so, an e-mail might do the trick—and save everyone a lot of time.
- Is there travel involved? An elevator ride is one thing; *real* travel is another. Whether the meeting will include attendees from across town or across the country, always stop and consider whether a conference call or webinar gathering might be just as effective (I use www.gotomeeting.com). Sometimes the

face-to-face is critical. Other times, it just doesn't matter, so why waste time and money traveling?

- What's your role in the meeting? Perhaps an assistant who takes good notes might be able to take your place. Just make sure that if decisions need to be made, the person filling in for you is capable of doing what's required. Others will be annoyed if your absence turns into an inconvenience.

- If you *do* need to be there personally, find out what's needed of you. Maybe only one item on a two-hour agenda involves you, so perhaps you can handle it and leave the meeting early. Or, ask what time you need to show up. Spending half of your day in meetings waiting for the matters that pertain to you can be a frustrating time waster.

Limit Attendees

More is *not* merrier when it comes to business meetings, so figure out who needs to be there. Don't worry about hurting someone's feelings if they aren't included. If you simply want to keep stakeholders or players in the loop, select their presence as optional instead of required. Always assume officers, directors—anyone higher up on the food chain—have much more profitable things to do than sit in your meeting. Consider how much people make and whether your meeting is worth an hour of their salary PLUS what they otherwise could have been doing if they weren't stuck there.

Only invite people if they have a direct contribution to make to the meeting objective, and/or if desired decisions can't be made without them. If their presence is only required for 10 minutes, give them the *first* 10 minutes, and then allow them to graciously depart.

Multiply Your Hands

Have meeting requests and responses go to your assistant (if you have one), not to you. Leave it to your admin to wade through all the responses. In Outlook, under Tools, Options, and Delegates, select "Send meeting requests and responses only to my delegates, not to me." Brilliant.

Avoid Meetings on Fridays

Many departments and teams decide as an informal policy to schedule meetings Monday–Thursday if at all possible. Too many people try to take long weekends or duck out early, which can make scheduling and rescheduling a nightmare on Fridays, plus you'll end up with a lot of no-shows. I try to leave Fridays open for personal appointments. I find if I put a doctor's appointment between business meetings, something always derails one or the other. It's hard to get my mind switched between different realms.

Distribute Your Agenda Early

Always send or request an agenda and include it in the text portion of the appointment or as an attachment. A basic agenda should include a statement of purpose, any logistical considerations, decisions to be made, a list of the topics to discuss (in priority order), who's responsible for the item, and time allotted for each. Ask participants to let you know in advance about any changes to the agenda items, so you can make adjustments if necessary. Once you get into the meeting, follow the agenda diligently, so you can ensure all points are covered, decisions are made, and the objectives are achieved.

Set Your Meeting's Length Yourself

Don't let Outlook pick the length of your meeting. The default is one hour, so guess how long most meetings are scheduled? Instead, match the length of the meeting to the purpose. If your agenda determines you'll only need 40 minutes, manually change the invitation and schedule it for that length of time. Otherwise, time will inherently expand to fill the amount available. On the other hand, if you promise to be out of there quickly, attendees will tend to work toward a goal. Slack time will prompt more socializing to naturally occur, and an hour will definitely get used. Some people try to build in buffer time—don't cave to this habit. I purposefully underschedule and announce the goal at the meeting's beginning to get everyone moving forward efficiently.

Use Online Scheduling for Outside Parties

According to international research of online scheduler Doodle .com, professionals spend five hours a week setting up meetings alone (see 1st International Study on Scheduling Trends 2009, www.doodle.com/about/mediareleases/survey.html). Doodle is a useful online polling tool to find a good day/time for participants to meet, and it is especially helpful for those who don't work at your company. I particularly like the Outlook plug-in that provides an online display of optional meeting times, allows all participants to indicate their preferred times, and enables the organizer to choose the final slot. It's very easily done, with no toggling between participants' calendars and no inefficient e-mail chains. Obtaining the availability of external parties is made effortless. Doodle makes scheduling transparent and flexible by engaging participants—regardless of whether they use online or offline calendars, paper planners, or no system at all.

Allow Enough Breaks

Provide at least one break for every hour and 15 minutes, max. Let attendees know at the outset what to expect. If you keep rambling on, and they aren't sure when they'll get a break, they'll just start getting up randomly and sneaking out. Clearly state at the beginning, "We'll meet from now until 10:00, and then we'll break until 10:10," and so forth. If you're meeting over a lunch hour, it's also common courtesy to provide food.

Be Considerate of Those in Other Time Zones

If you're in the Pacific zone, and some of your meeting participants are calling in from the Eastern zone, a 2:00 meeting puts them into departure time. People may have child-care commitments at the end of the day. Similarly, an early morning meeting on the east coast can severely inconvenience folks on the west coast and reduce the odds of attendance.

Strike a Balance on Scheduling

Scheduling a meeting too far out often elicits a bunch of cancellations and requests to reschedule as you get closer. It also increases the chance you'll get trumped by someone higher up. However, on the other side of the coin, if you wait to schedule a meeting until the last minute, it's hard to find a block of time when most people are readily available. I find it's best to schedule two to three weeks in advance. Anything sooner or further off is fraught with scheduling challenges and conflicts.

Immediately Inform the Meeting Leader of Conflicts

If you have a change in your calendar but don't want to "rock the boat," you inconvenience more people the longer you wait. It takes effort to work schedules around appointments, so as soon as you know, raise the flag. The chair can determine if the meeting can proceed without you or if it needs to be moved.

Confirm Everything

I've occasionally shown up for a meeting to discover the other person "forgot." Although it's nice to assume that all adults are responsible and will do what they say they'll do, it's always a good idea to dash off a quick e-mail beforehand: "Looking forward to seeing you on (date) at (time) at (location). Let me know if something comes up." I don't treat people like kindergartners and try to make them confirm the details are correct (my dentist's office does this—and it makes me crazy). I simply request a call if there's been a change.

You also want to make sure you get and map out any directions well in advance of running out the door. I look at my calendar for the next day before I leave work to make sure I'm ready to roll first thing in the morning. Confirm with attendees for your meetings as well; simply open the original meeting request, select Actions, and then New Message to Attendees.

Journal Your Meeting Notes

Many people don't know how to use the Journal feature in Outlook, or even what it's for. If you've ever accidentally clicked it, you'll get a pop-up box asking you if you're *sure* you want to turn on the Journal. Most people freak out and click No. Next time, click Yes. Open a new Journal entry, select Meeting in the Type dropdown, and type up your meeting notes. Then, input the meeting's day/time, indicate in the Contacts field who attended, select a Category for the meeting name or project—and save. When you pull up a Contact and click the Activities tab or button, you'll be able to see the Journal entries (notes) from every meeting you've ever had with the Contact. You can also pull up your Journal entries by Category to review meeting notes as far back as you'd like. Or give your notes to your assistant, have him type them up in the text field of the original meeting notice, save, and send a message to attendees (under Actions). The Journal also documents conversations, phone calls, faxes sent, and so on.

Scheduling Meetings

Do you find it's close to impossible to get five or more attendees available at the same time and the same date? When key players are overbooked, it can take hours just to schedule a single meeting. Here are three questions you should ask yourself in regards to attendees whenever you schedule a meeting:

- *Do we really need all these people?* Make sure you aren't inviting anyone who doesn't need to have a seat at the table. Not only does it make scheduling more difficult, but you'll either (1) waste their time or (2) bend over backward to accommodate someone who isn't going to show up anyway.
- *Can we keep people in the loop without inviting them to every meeting?* Some meetings are full of wallflowers who need to know what's going on, but they don't necessarily need to contribute. Publishing meeting minutes or distributing essential information electronically can condense time and the attendee list. Also, take a look to see if some work areas are sending multiple representatives.

Choosing a single designee from each area allows you to have everyone represented without physically being in the room.

- *Do we need to meet at all?* This is a question you should ask about *every* meeting, not just the hard-to-schedule ones. Any meeting without a clear objective (if not a formal agenda) should be on the chopping block.

Develop Effective Teleconferencing Guidelines

Your marketing team is based in Chicago; you work from your home office in Denver; and the salespeople work from remote field sites all over the globe. You need to connect to discuss next quarter's sales efforts and don't have the budget to travel to a central location. Teleconference—or webinar—to the rescue!

Teleconferences can be a great way to connect virtual teams from around the world. They're less expensive than face-to-face meetings; often take less time; and allow teams to communicate more informally, ask questions, and solve problems better than e-mail can.

Holding a virtual meeting *should* be a no-brainer. What can be so hard about a group of people talking on the phone? All you have to do is connect everyone and make decisions as if you were in person, right? There's the dilemma: This is *not* your normal phone call. A teleconference is a meeting. To pull it off, you'll have to do more than pick up the phone; you'll have to prepare for it in the same way you would a meeting, with a few extra details. It's especially complex if some participants are meeting face-to-face while others are remote.

To make sure your next teleconference is successful, follow the three Ps (mnemonics again—I promise, they work!) of effective teleconferencing:

1. *Planning.* You must prepare for a teleconference like any other meeting. Include the following items in your planning:
   - Coordinating the calendars of several busy people for a teleconference can take days. Give yourself a couple of weeks before the desired meeting day to find a time convenient for all.

- A teleconference can become unmanageable with more than 10 people, so try to limit the number of participants to those whose presence is truly required. Include people who can make a significant contribution, and copy or make optional those who need to know what's happening on the minutes following the call.
- One week prior to the meeting, solicit input for items to add to the agenda. Send out a detailed meeting agenda specifying the meeting objective and decisions to be made at least two days prior to the call. Don't forget to send all documents, notes, and prework or required reading.
- Keep the process simple and the schedule short. Most people can't pay attention while listening and staring out into space for more than about 30 minutes and will begin checking e-mail. If you have more issues than time, plan several teleconferences to discuss different goals.
- Include the teleconference phone number and PIN number with the messages one week before the meeting; again, two days before the meeting; and on the day of the meeting.
- Test out the teleconferencing equipment days prior to the actual meeting. Conduct a few trial runs with the other locations, to ensure you can hear them and they you. Surprises are no fun on the day of the meeting, when frustrated participants have to sit around while you troubleshoot the equipment.

2. *Process.* These are all the things you do to conduct an effective teleconference during the meeting:

- The person who calls the meeting can act as the "voice traffic controller," or another person may be appointed. The facilitator is responsible for keeping the meeting on track. That person notes the topic to be discussed, based on the timed agenda, and asks specific people to report.
- Before you speak, remember that some people may not recognize your voice. Even if you think, "Everyone knows me," always begin with "This is Laura," and then speak. When you pick up the conversation again, repeat, "This is Laura again."
- Don't be afraid of silence. Since the phone is devoid of facial expressions, you can't always read emotion. Someone may be formulating a question in his or her mind and needs another

minute to chime in. Silence doesn't always imply consent or completion. Make sure someone has finished speaking before you begin, or you'll always end up interrupting others midsentence.

- If a group of people is meeting in the same room, with other remote sites dialing in, try to make the virtual participants feel included. If someone cracks a joke and the group bursts out with laughter, let the others know who said what and repeat the joke.

3. *Protocol.* These are the guidelines and rules of etiquette and engagement for participants to follow:

- Use the "mute" feature of the phone or teleconferencing system when you're not speaking, so participants can't hear the airport music or your dog. Some systems allow the facilitator to mute all participants, taking them off mute to ask or respond to questions.

- Be present. "I'm sorry, could you repeat the question?" is an all-too-common phrase heard during calls, which basically announces you weren't paying attention. Don't risk looking unprofessional; stay focused. Be there now. As good as you think you are at multitasking, the conscious mind isn't capable of reading e-mail and listening to a speaker at exactly the same time. Surfing the net or using the mute button to carry on another conversation effectively removes you from the meeting.

- Keep side conversations to a minimum. It's frustrating as a remote teleconference participant to hear babbling in the background. It makes it difficult to distinguish the actual speaker from the other noise, and there's a constant echo on the line.

- Read all prework and be prepared to participate actively in the conversation. Even though you can't be seen, your voice and presence—albeit virtual—will be missed if you're silent.

Sorry, He's in a Meeting

Although meetings can seem like the bane of personal productivity, we couldn't do business without them. It's one of the ironies of modern professional life. E-mail and a quick phone call can only do so much. Face-to-face—or at least voice-to-voice—contact for minutes or hours at a time is necessary to achieve the synergetic interactions that drive accomplishment.

That doesn't make it any less frustrating to spend half your day in meetings and meeting preparations when you're trying to get things done. Although this might *be* productivity to a corporate cog living for 5:00 PM on Friday, to the SuperCompetent among us, it's a potential intrusion on our productive time, because it requires that we give up something else to make progress. After all, they're not making days any longer yet; all you have is 24 hours.

You can tame the meeting monster and your availability if you try, but you'll need to be proactive about it. Apply these handy tips, and I guarantee you'll not only save time for yourself, you'll save it for other people, too.

SUMMARY: AVAILABILITY

Availability is a loaded word, at least in business terms. It means so much more than just being there; any decent worker can and should be there for their employers, subordinates, and co-workers when they're needed. SuperCompetent people need to be keenly aware of time management and being there too much. After all, we each have a limited amount of time, and we're not going to get any more.

Saying yes to everything will leave you so overburdened that you won't be available when people really *do* need you—except on those rare occasions when you manage to clear a task off your schedule. You require some flexibility, which means you not only have to learn how to say no to some requests (or creatively negotiate them somewhat), but you also need to learn how to deal with the distractions and diversions commanding all your time.

You don't have to do everything, by any means; the idea is to be SuperCompetent, not SuperHuman. Superman is a fantasy, and even if he wasn't, you have to remember he's supposed to be an alien from another planet, *not* a human being. Knowing how to delegate and/or outsource tasks whenever you can—and having the wisdom to do so—is a must.

You'll also need to learn effective scheduling techniques to make life easier for you and everyone else, and hone them to maximum effectiveness, so things don't get out of hand. The same is true when it comes to meetings. Meetings are a prime example of the tendency for tasks to expand to fill the amount of time available.

You don't have to let time stealers eat into your productivity. Stand up, step up, and take back your time!

Go to www.TheProductivityPro.com/Availability to receive bonus material, the SuperCompetent Key 2 assessment questions, a summary, and the action-planning worksheet in Microsoft Word format. Get additional resources, audios, videos, and more at www.SuperCompetentBook.com.

ACTION PLANNING WORKSHEET: AVAILABILITY

6. I refuse requests when appropriate; I know how to say no graciously.
   What came to mind when I read this?

   _____

   _____

   _____

   _____

   What is my action plan for improvement?

   _____

   _____

   _____

   _____

7. I set appropriate boundaries and protect my time from others.
   What came to mind when I read this?

   _____

   _____

   _____

   _____

   What is my action plan for improvement?

   _____

   _____

   _____

   _____

8. I push tasks down to the lowest level of responsibility, trusting others to do their jobs.
   What came to mind when I read this?

   _____
   _____
   _____
   _____

   What is my action plan for improvement?

   _____
   _____
   _____
   _____

9. I schedule my day realistically according to my key activities.
   What came to mind when I read this?

   _____
   _____
   _____
   _____

   What is my action plan for improvement?

   _____
   _____
   _____
   _____

10. I weigh the results of attending each meeting against the alternative results I could produce instead.
    What came to mind when I read this?

    _____
    _____
    _____
    _____

    What is my action plan for improvement?

    _____
    _____
    _____
    _____

PART 3

SuperCompetent Key 3: Attention

SuperCompetent people focus intently on their important Activities during their Available time.

ATTENTION is the capacity to concentrate.

This key allows you to filter or tune out environmental distractions unrelated to your current task.

Sylvia V. Francis, Senior Professional in Human Resources (SPHR)—someone to whom I'm connected on LinkedIn—recently wrote to me: "The folks who succeed in my environment are focused on: Getting the job done, their department's success, their company's success, the success of their own career; most importantly, they are *not* focused on the negative chat around the proverbial water cooler, whining and moaning about belt-tightening measures or how they're going to get the job done with less resources. They are proud of what they have accomplished at the end of each day."

Hear, hear! Sylvia's statement is a perfect introduction to the third key of the SuperCompetent pro: Attention. When you're working on an important proposal that must be completed by the end of the day, you need to give it your focused efforts to finish the task. So many other things compete for our attention and tempt us to do "just this one little thing." Switching from one thing to another distracts us from our primary task—and forces us to stay later to finish it. You need a great deal of discipline to concentrate on a single undertaking without being diverted by something more enjoyable (oooooh, shiny penny).

Many of the distractions seem to be packaged in some form of technology. Anyone who works in the business world knows technology can be both a blessing and a curse. At its best, it allows us to do more in less time; at its worst, it's a frustrating, productivity-draining distraction. As we rely more and more on our various gizmos and gadgets, productivity can become a tricky thing. It's like the prescription drugs they advertise on TV. Sure, the stuff works as advertised, but just listen to all those side effects!

CHAPTER 11

Don't Open That!

SUPERCOMPETENT Hero Thinking:	I don't read each e-mail when it arrives; I'm able to stay focused on my work.
SIMPLY COMPETENT Zero Thinking:	This is getting boring. Cool, another e-mail; I'll just check it really fast.

Do you keep one eye on your inbox all day long? What does that do to your productivity? Let's face it: E-mail can be a phenomenal productivity tool, but *it can eat your day alive* if you let it. Dropping everything and attending to every e-mail that comes in throughout the day derails your productivity over and over again. Not only do you waste whatever time it takes for you to read, ignore, or act on a given e-mail message; it also takes time to refocus your attention on whatever you were doing prior to the interruption. Lots of people insist their overflowing inbox is beyond their control, but as a SuperCompetent, you must take steps to start getting a handle on it right away.

Control the Reflex

Remember Pavlov? In his famous experiment, he gave his dog a treat every time he rang a bell. Eventually the dog would salivate as soon as he heard the bell; it was a learned response. Every time our e-mail alerts go off, we salivate. Unfortunately, the reward isn't there, since the majority of incoming e-mail is junk. Out of every 10 e-mails you receive, how many are *really* important? One? None? E-mail has become the master, and we are the servants. Bring an egg timer from home and set it for 30 minutes. If you can't stop thinking about your e-mail, you're addicted—a big productivity problem.

As a society, workers are addicted to e-mail. Countless professionals sit at their desks, slaves to the Send/Receive button, waiting for the next trigger that prompts their Pavlovian response to interrupt whatever they're doing and check it. An unopened e-mail! Someone loves me. Forget that important project! Your Obsessive Compulsive E-mail Disorder (OCED) kicks in. You . . . just . . . can't . . . help . . . it . . . and you check.

Many workers allow themselves to get sucked into the e-mail vortex for an entire day and don't complete any actual work. We blame the sheer mass of e-mail for sucking away all our time, rather than acknowledging the reality: Your e-mail is controlling you.

If you don't turn things around and learn to control the different technologies that vie for your attention—e-mail, the phone ringing, your cell phone buzzing, and instant messages popping up on the screen—you've got a recipe for disaster.

It's partially the fault of our software settings. In Microsoft Outlook, users receive *four* different alerts every time an e-mail is received: A sound goes off; the mouse cursor briefly changes; an envelope appears in the system tray; and a Desktop Alert pops up. Oh my goodness—it's no wonder we can't get anything done.

But it's partly our own fault as well, because we respond to these e-mails as they come in, regardless of their priority. Accounting professionals use a term called FIFO: First In, First Out. This is how most people handle e-mail. You were busy all day responding to urgent requests, and you're mysteriously tired, but you didn't get anything done.

Take Back Everyday Activities

Just as technology can interfere with personal time, it can also wreak havoc with your productivity during normal working hours. Yes, you can set your e-mail to tell you the instant a new message arrives. No, you shouldn't drop every e-mail as it comes in.

Think about it. How many e-mails do you get in a single day? If you're constantly checking your e-mail, you're constantly interrupting otherwise productive activities to deal with issues, which 99 times out of 100, aren't important. Even if it only takes you a second to read a message, you're still derailing your train of thought and wasting several minutes to get back on track. You don't answer it anyway, leaving it in your inbox and adding to the stream-of-consciousness thinking in your head.

You'll be amazed at how much you can get done when you say no to all the little technological distractions competing for your attention.

- *Turn off your e-mail alerts.* Go to your Tools menu in Outlook, select Options, then E-mail Options, and Advanced E-mail Options. You'll see "When a new e-mail arrives in my box, do the following." Uncheck all those boxes.
- *Close Outlook completely.* If you absolutely, positively can't resist glancing at your e-mail inbox, shut down Outlook completely. Turning off your alerts will prevent the envelope in the system tray from constantly reminding you there's e-mail waiting.
- *Check at regular intervals, as few times as possible.* I don't believe it's realistic to only check once a day, but you shouldn't be checking it 27 times a day, either. Find a balance in responding to your colleagues and using self-control to get your important work accomplished.
- *Schedule work periods.* Close your Outlook, put your IM on DND, forward your calls to voicemail, turn off your handheld, and shut down all technology, which will give you a period of time to concentrate. The big differentiating factor is control. Create a bubble of silence around yourself.

Schlimmbesserung Revisited

E-mail is an important part of any business environment, but it shouldn't take up your entire life. An e-mail message isn't a toy for you to play with; it's *work*. Of course, you will have to deal with e-mail throughout the day, and sometimes it's going to be worth handling. But don't let the mundane messages suck you in and claim time you should be spending doing activities of greater value. The same goes for all other handy technology: It's there to help you get things done, not help you play hooky.

CHAPTER 12

eBay and Yahoo! and YouTube, Oh My!

SUPERCOMPETENT Hero Thinking:	I leave distractions for my downtime.
SIMPLY COMPETENT Zero Thinking:	I'd better get to work; I have a lot to do today—hey, I wonder how I'm doing on eBay? It'll only take a minute to check . . .

The most effective time-management system in the world won't do a thing to improve your productivity if you don't focus on the task at hand. For many of us, the problem isn't a lack of will-power; it's having the restraint to refuse fun.

Make no mistake: Productivity in the workplace is under attack. *Business Week* explored the issue in a 2008 article that reported on the effects of technological distractions in the work-place. The gist of their findings shows the average American office worker spends about 28 percent of the workday on distractions, which ranged from reading personal e-mail to checking out funny videos on YouTube. As a SuperCompetent, this can't be typical of you.

If every worker spent an hour a day on Facebook, what would be the equivalent salary per person . . . across your entire company . . . multiplied by all U.S. companies? It would cause businesses to lose billions each year—exactly why some companies have been forced to block certain sites.

The Internet is a bottomless pit of information—some useful and some not so useful. It's much too easy to sit down to do one thing (pay a bill, look up an address) and end up wasting time on something else entirely (reading news stories or checking your social networking profiles).

If you find meandering around the Web to be relaxing, fine; just make sure you do it at an appropriate time and place that doesn't interfere with work or family time. Otherwise, treat the Internet like any other tool: Use it when you need it and put it away when you're done.

It Starts at Home with the Television

Why is it we can spend all day scrounging for extra minutes and then head home, only to flush countless hours down the drain watching television? Television—even bad television—can be habit-forming. One show can lead to another and end up turning your half-hour escape into an entire evening wasted. You stay up late to watch your favorite show. Exhausted in the morning, you head to work. Great productivity strategy, eh?

According to an American Time Use survey from the U.S. Bureau of Labor Statistics, the average person spends 2.7 hours a day watching television. In other studies, Americans say television is the least necessary part of their lives, yet we devote more time to it than to any other leisure activity. We estimate we have 16 hours of free time a week, yet we also report watching 21 hours of television a week. It's not hard to see where some of the time is flying. *Newsday* columnist Diane Werts put it this way: "I began to see how television, watched wantonly, can start to suck the life out of your life. You start to think its lightning pace, snap judgments, and emotional manipulation is the way life inevitably works. I feel like constant watching has rewired my body clock." Personally, I watch *no* television. Yes, you read that right—zero. Okay, except once annually for the Country Music Awards (CMAs). I'm not criticizing those who do, but it must be purposeful. I get my news through other mediums.

Take a quick inventory of the last few television shows you watched. Think about how many you thought about in advance and purposefully sat down to enjoy. Now think about how many you ended up watching just "because they were on."

Here's a better strategy: Pick a few shows you enjoy and watch them each week. TiVo or otherwise record them, so you can skip the commercials and watch whenever you'd like. Don't stay up until 11:00 waiting for your favorite late night show to come up. After watching, shut the TV off and go on about your business!

Remember, we have more free time than we had in the past; we simply don't realize it. Maybe it's because virtually all the added leisure gained over the last 30 years has been spent in front of the TV and the Internet, that series of tubes. The increase in television watching has cut into the time we have allocated to almost everything else in our lives—but most especially to activities outside the home, like clubs, sports, religious observances, and parties.

As we devote more time to television, we seem to appreciate it less. It becomes more habit than entertainment. And if you spend more of your leisure doing an activity you only marginally enjoy, it will contribute to your sense of lost time. It's a poor practice and makes no logical sense.

So where's the fine line between best utilizing technology and being consumed by it? Here are four simple guidelines to follow to make the most of technology:

1. *Make purposeful decisions around its use. Purposefully* choose to open a browser or turn on the television. Do it by design, not by default. Don't use it as a method of procrastinating on something more important.
2. *Get what you need.* Decide to what degree you want to embrace technology. We need to find a happy medium between staying ahead of the technological curve and being left in the dust. Although many employees don't need handhelds, they do need the tools to do their jobs without getting bogged down. If you are wasting time with dial-up modems or dinosaur computers, it's time to invest in technology that won't hold you back. Buy your staff BlackBerries if they request it—even if they aren't at the approved level—if they believe it will help them be more productive. Or open your wallet and buy one yourself.

3. *Get the training you need.* Once you have the technology, learn how to use it. You'd be amazed at all the capabilities and features contained in software—such as Outlook—that most people will never use in their working lives. I'd estimate most people know how to use 10 to 20 percent of the capabilities in Outlook, GroupWise, Lotus Notes, and so forth. Learn how to get the most from the tools you use every day. Invest in yourself and your team.

4. *Manage expectations.* Once you have the tools you need to get the job done, it's important to set expectations around how they'll be used. What's a reasonable time frame to expect a reply to an e-mail? How often should we be checking our voicemails? Should we be reachable by cell at all hours of the day and night? The answers don't matter much (though, in general, less is more), but coming up with clear, unequivocal expectations does. Once you have the tools to be productive, you can be sure you're using them in a way that makes sense for your organization.

How Now, Technogeek?

Technology is a tool—a means to an end—not the end itself. It's become far too easy in the modern workplace to let technology monopolize our time. Though these days, it's our wonderful electronics that hold us in thrall, you can bet it traces right back to hand-cranked adding machines and typewriters—or heck, cuneiform and clay tablets. *Schlimmbesserung, schlimmbesserung!* If Charles Babbage had been able to perfect his Difference Engine back in the 1840s, a substantial portion of us would probably be slaves to implanted electronics and brain computers keeping us in constant contact with our work sphere by now—whether we liked it or not. Thank goodness it hasn't happened—yet—right?

Many of us feel it has. But this isn't a technocracy quite yet; we do have the option of turning our technology off and ignoring it when it's beneficial to do so. So *do it.*

CHAPTER 13

The Harder I Work, the Behinder I Get!

SUPERCOMPETENT Hero Thinking:	I can only do one thing at a time, so I limit my multi-tasking to maximize my productivity.
SIMPLY COMPETENT Zero Thinking:	If I do a whole bunch of things at once, I can get more done!

Multitasking has become a beloved word in professional circles. However, the most recent data on this concept suggests we should take a closer look. A study in multitasking by Cornell University psychology professor Morton Christiansen and NIH research fellow Christopher Conway found people can multitask fairly well when they use different senses to complete tasks. For example, you can drive while keeping an eye on traffic and listening to the radio at the same time, or chop up vegetables while you're talking on the phone. However, when similar stimuli compete for the same senses at the same time—such as two people talking to you at once—jams our perceptual frequencies. This is why, as parents, we always intuitively say to our children, "One at a time, please." So if you're trying to pay attention to two different technologies at once, such as a phone call and e-mail, your brain slows to a crawl, and you drain a ton of energy trying to concentrate.

Multitasked to Overwhelmed

Let's look at the typical champion multitasker's day, based on an actual report by a colleague who works from home:

Wake up; get ready; watch the news; go to the office; fax the counter-signed agreement back to the client; pay the water bill; make a cup of coffee; let the dog out to pee; return Mom's e-mail; let the dog back in; Google high school sweetheart; return best friend's e-mail; check favorite blogs for new postings; call Sprint to find out where your $29 rebate is; return e-mail; answer the phone—Hi Mom, yes I did return your e-mail, no it should be there, go to Inbox, Mom, I'm going to have to call you back; oops there's the doorbell—UPS—sign for the package; as long as I'm up I may as well get another cup of coffee; oh my gosh, this kitchen's a mess.

When 5:00 rolled around, my colleague was exhausted and felt he'd accomplished nothing of substance. There was no time left to talk to a client; make a deal; start a marketing campaign; or write a book—you know—the activities that actually bring in revenue. This is precisely why we sometimes find ourselves wondering, "Why, if I've been working and working and working *all day,* am I still . . . not . . . rich?" Easy; you concentrated your efforts on unimportant tasks, and now you don't have the energy necessary to move your career forward.

Do you know how I *know* when I'm exhausted? When I'm in the hotel room the morning of a speaking engagement, reach for the mouthwash, take a swig, and realize it's the *bath gel.* When I want to call one of my children, and I run through the names of all of them, my pets, and best friend before you get to the right one: James, Johnny, Emma, Faith, Rachel, Darla—MEAGAN! When I take a quart of Ben and Jerry's Chunky Monkey out of the freezer, serve myself, and put it back . . . in the pantry. By the way, those aren't hypothetical examples. I've done each and every one of them. I'm not proud of it; I'm just being honest.

Do you feel that way? You're running around from place to place, task to task, and you're exhausted. It's just too much. So what can you do? You can refocus where you spend your mental and emotional energy.

If You Think It, Ink It

Here's one thing that I learned from my Dad (whom I called Daddykins) that you can start doing immediately. Daddykins always kept a little Mead spiral notebook in his shirt pocket (which he referred to as his brain), and would say, "If you think it, ink it." "If you think it, ink it." Okay, you just heard it twice, and you're probably *already* annoyed. I heard it almost every day of my life, and it used to drive me crazy. Turns out—and I hate to admit this—Daddykins was right.

If you keep a planner, notebook, pocket recorder, or a handheld—any tool that works for you—handy, and you're trying to focus on an important task and get a random thought—you don't *do* it, you *note* it. "Ooh, I should call so-and-so; oooh, what a great idea; oooh, I should send this e-mail . . ." But *don't do it* right then, because you're in the middle of something else. Instead, you capture it—on paper or electronically—and go right back to the important task.

Here's the cool part: When you write something down, your brain *thinks* you did it. In essence, your brain checks it off. You no longer have to expend energy trying to remember things, and you can concentrate on the task at hand. When you're through with your task, you have a list of things to do. You'll discover this is a great little trick for managing your mental energy.

Metacognition: Get Above It All

Metacognition can be a difficult subject to grasp—perhaps because, ironically, it seems absurdly simple when you boil it down to what truly matters. Basically, metacognition involves thinking about thinking or knowing about knowing. It's how you shape your thoughts in order to better achieve your ends. It also involves learning how to become a better learner. This is why any form of education is a prime example of metacognition, but it doesn't stop there. Whenever you sit down and plan out how to approach a task, or perform any action to monitor your comprehension or progress toward completing the task, you're employing meta-cognition. School projects, quizzes, and tests are metacognitive undertakings, as is homework. In fact, formal education generally consists of one metacognitive task after another.

Effective metacognition requires the following factors: (1) specific factual or declarative knowledge (i.e., knowing *what*); (2) conditional or contextual knowledge (knowing *when* and *why*); and (3) procedural or methodological knowledge (knowing *how*). Good metacognologists maintain a more varied toolkit of learning responses than other people. They tend to do well at most tasks because they're flexible, less likely to be distracted by unimportant details, and self-regulated. That is, they take initiative without undue prodding and are more apt to choose the right tools for the job.

For example, my daughter Meagan—who's currently 15 years old—has discovered she performs worse on tests when she studies while keeping Facebook open. She forces herself to keep it shut when an important test is looming, which is a good example of metacognition: Using your knowledge of the way you think to *shape* the way you behave. She is third in her class of 450+, partially due to these habits of self-control (and partially because she's brilliant . . . not that I'm biased).

Metacognition may come into play in the following workplace situations:

- Planning how to break a large task down into more manageable subtasks.
- Creating and maintaining to-do lists.
- Creating and maintaining business systems and processes.
- Following quality management standards like those mandated under ISO-9000 or Six Sigma.
- Performing self-assessments to determine how far along you are on a particular task or learning situation.
- Creating periodic progress reports for others.
- Coordinating large projects involving numerous personnel.

Each case requires that you use logic and planning—your ability to *think*—to either assess your progress on a particular task or to guide how you're going to think about it in the future. True metacognition is all about self-regulating your thinking and learning, and it lies at the root of just about any work you'll ever do that rises above the level of unskilled labor. It's not something you only do occasionally; the SuperCompetent should exercise metacognitive abilities every single day.

Stop the Self-Sabotage

Is there a single serious professional out there who *doesn't* want to be more productive? I doubt it. So it's no wonder we multitask constantly. To some extent, multitasking is necessary in the sense that we all have to juggle multiple projects and activities at any particular time. However, trying too hard to do too many things *at one time* is simply counterproductive.

It's easier to concentrate if your mind isn't scrambled, so make sincere efforts to focus on just a few important things at a time. Go beyond trimming your multitasking list. Learn to cut through the clutter and control distractions, instead of letting distractions control you. Stop trying to do everything at once. If you think it, ink it, and come back to it later: Don't drop what you're doing and pursue the new line of thought. Put the metacognitive techniques into play so you can have time enough to concentrate.

CHAPTER 14

Socializing for Success

SUPERCOMPETENT Hero Thinking:	I don't allow socializing to overwhelm my productivity, whether online or in real life.
SIMPLY COMPETENT Zero Thinking:	I'll just leave the Facebook window open, so my friends can IM me throughout the day.

Having children has shown me that it truly is a whole new world out there. When my daughter entered high school, she joined the choir and met a boy we'll call Chris. One week later, she received a "Relationship Request" in Facebook from him, which she accepted. Yes, you read that right: Instead of talking or calling or e-mailing or even texting, this generation of teens asks each other to go steady by sending a relationship request on Facebook. A few weeks later, Meagan broke up with Chris by removing the relationship link.

Let me explain. You can indicate on your Facebook profile whether you're married, single, or in a relationship. If you're friends with a person, you can claim to be in a relationship with that person and tag him/her; then Facebook sends a notification to the other person, asking for verification of that relationship. If you accept, that person now shows up on your Facebook profile, hyperlinked, for all your friends to see and click on to find out about your boyfriend. Mind-boggling but true. This generation is coming . . . into your workplace . . . computer savvy and wired.

However, social networking sites like Facebook aren't just for kids anymore. Web 2.0 has revolutionized online communication. Gone are the days of static web sites; LinkedIn, Facebook, YouTube, podcasting and a multitude of social bookmarking sites are here to stay. Businesses and individuals worldwide keep finding interesting ways to use these kinds of interactive online media to do some pretty amazing things, from building their brands to getting to know their customers. However, while social networks and other tools are great resources, they're lousy masters. Social media can be a double-edged sword: While it can help you make connections and expand your organization's reach, it can also decrease your productivity if you're not careful. You could spend all day hopping around to different sites, updating your information, and connecting with people all over the world. But how does the activity add to your daily efficiency?

Here are some ideas you can start using right away to help you use social media efficiently and productively.

Separate Your Business and Personal Lives

Not only is this a good idea in terms of maintaining professionalism and not boring your friends; it also has big implications for productivity. If you comingle your personal and professional social networking, you're inviting your friends and family into your workday and your clients into your personal life. When you're at work and decide to focus, for example, on marketing yourself or an event, you'll almost certainly be distracted by updates and messages from family and friends. Just glancing through those personal posts is going to make your social media activities take a lot longer than they need to.

I use Twitter (www.twitter.com/laurastack), a Facebook Fan Page (not my personal profile) at www.facebook.com/productivitypro and LinkedIn (www.linkedin.com/in/laurastack) for my business network (clients, prospects, vendors). I use Facebook for my personal network (*actual* friends, family, speaker buddies). I do have a Productivity Pro® tip of the day that gets posted to both, but the rest is separate. I announce business seminars, news, and updates on LinkedIn, and I put personal updates on

Facebook without having to wonder what a client might think. Instead of friending my clients, I invite them to click LIKE on my Laura Stack Fan Page instead, so I can choose what business items to post separate from my personal wall. If I'm talking about the glass of wine I just had, I don't have to worry about what my clients will think. I only visit Facebook when I'm on personal time, rather than thinking of it as a marketing activity.

Get Into a Regular Social Media Routine

Keeping current on social networks doesn't take much time, provided you approach it efficiently. You could easily spend the better part of an afternoon reading blog posts and checking status updates, but generally speaking, that's not why you're there. In fact, the activities that eat up the most time are typically not the ones that add value at all; they're just another form of procrastination, like lingering at a coworker's desk or surfing the Web.

Instead of allowing this to occur, build a social media routine and establish dedicated blocks of time to handle it. This might be a single 15-minute session each morning or a few quick ones spread throughout the day—whatever meets your needs and situation. If you keep the time period short, you'll be more likely to maintain focus and accomplish what you logged on to do, and less likely to fritter away time with idle chat or mindless wandering.

Or you can do what I did: Write a year's worth of postings at one time. Yes, I wrote 365 daily Productivity Pro® tips over the course of a couple of focused days. Now I don't have to think of something brilliant to say each day. I currently have over 3,200 Twitter followers who are interested in these tips (I don't post these manually . . . read on to find out how).

Embrace Third-Party Applications to Automate Manual Processes

If you've determined it makes good business sense for you to participate in several social media platforms, it won't be long before you realize just how big a time commitment it is to keep each one current. It was hard enough back when we just had to keep our web sites and blogs up to date; these days, that's just the beginning. Chances are you're going to need a little help at some point.

This is where third-party applications come in. Rather than taking the time to post to multiple places, tools like Ping.fm allow you to go to one site to update all your social networking sites. This saves you the trouble of hopping from one site to another and generally streamlines the experience across the board.

To get even fancier, you can load your future postings into HootSuite.com, which will update Ping, which then updates Twitter, Facebook, LinkedIn, del.icio.us, Typepad, AIM, GTalk, MySpace, and so forth. That means that it can keep your account looking alive even while you're sitting in a meeting. You obviously don't want to be disingenuous with such a tool, but it's perfect for reminding followers of special events, sharing professional wisdom, or anything else more strategic than a simple status update.

I also like the assistance that SocialOomph.com (formerly TweetLater) provides in managing multiple accounts. It also offers a number of business tools to help you leverage social media effectively. For example, it automatically follows back anyone who follows you on Twitter with a custom message. I also get a daily digest of keywords I'm searching for on Twitter. Lastly, blip.tv is a video uploading site, which posts to YouTube, TubeMogul, iTunes, your blog, and so on, and provides the Really Simple Syndication (RSS) feed.

I definitely recommend at least checking out Ping, HootSuite, SocialOomph, and Blip.tv. Your specific needs and personal tastes will influence which platforms make sense for you, but the best way to learn about them is to give them a try.

Decide What You're Trying to Do

The biggest reason otherwise productive, well-intentioned people end up wasting a ton of time on social networks is that they never sit down and figure out what they want to accomplish with these tools in the first place. It isn't just about how many friends, followers, or readers you have; it's about what your career or your business has to gain. That might mean interacting with existing clients, reaching out to new prospects, or simply building your online reputation.

Have a goal in mind whenever you commit yourself to another online profile. Otherwise, you could spend 40 hours a week bouncing from one thing to another without ever adding real value to your business or career. Meaningful goals might be based on sales (establishing one new lead per week), generating awareness (post industry-related content once per day), or even something more subjective, such as establishing a reputation as a valuable online resource for customers and prospects. Be clear on what you're trying to accomplish. After all, if your goal is simply to create an account and make some noise, then that's all you'll do.

Connect, Listen, and Contribute

This is the easiest one to forget. If you've already decided to invest time and energy into social networking, don't forget you aren't there to simply broadcast your sales pitch to anyone who'll listen. Just as you make time to Tweet, update a Facebook fan page, or post on LinkedIn, you need to set aside a few minutes to see what other people are saying. This will give you great insights into the needs of the community and help you better focus your message when you *do* have something to say. Even carving out just five minutes twice a day to pop in on others' platforms and profiles can add tremendous value to your social networking activities.

For example, Twitter provides plenty of great opportunities to listen, but realistically, this social media network, famous for broadcasting what millions of users are eating for lunch, *does* come with its fair share of background noise and low-value information. Third-party applications like Twitter Lists, TweetDeck, and Twhirl can help you scan, sort, and filter the conversations taking place on Twitter and hone in on important postings without wasting time on the inane. If I were to just scan the tweets of everyone I'm following, I'd be overwhelmed by mundane updates ("eating lunch"), annoying promotions ("retweet to win XYZ"), and complete nonsense ("which Harry Potter character are you?"). Twitter and Facebook lists, TweetDeck, and Twhirl allow me to focus on the handful of people I know well. I can keep an eye on important topics through search terms like *productive* or *time management*, or *high potentials*—which saves time and keeps me focused.

Back to Work, You!

Social media has added a whole new dimension to our professional and social lives and made it much easier to combine the two— which is not always a good thing. If you use social media in your business, remember it's there to help, *not* to take over your life. Clamp down on your tendencies to oversocialize. Contribute and use Social Media to your advantage but don't descend into silliness. Who cares if you're listening to Culture Club or eating a tuna sandwich right this minute? Aren't you supposed to be doing something productive? Remember, SuperCompetents do not post ridiculous updates.

Hopefully I've given you some food for thought as you pursue the social media endeavors that make sense for you and your career. I also hope you'll drop me a line out there in the social media sphere.

Follow me: www.twitter.com/laurastack
Link in: www.linkedin.com/in/laurastack
Like me: www.facebook.com/ProductivityPro
YouTube: www.youtube.com/theproductivitypro
Read my blog: www.theproductivitypro.com/blog

CHAPTER 15

BlackBerry/ CrackBerry

SUPERCOMPETENT Hero Thinking:	I know technology and my handheld are tools to help me be more productive—no addiction here.
SIMPLY COMPETENT Zero Thinking:	Wow, look at all the cool apps for my iPhone! I need to download this one, and this one, and this one . . .

I have a friend who jokes that there are always three people in her bed: herself, her husband, and her BlackBerry. A recent study confirmed people do indeed love their BlackBerries. According to an online article on WCBSTV.com (http://wcbstv.com/ technology/BlackBerry.pda.sheraton.2.818223.html), "The study of 6,500 traveling executives says 35 percent of them would choose their PDA over their spouse." Wait a minute—people would choose a communications device over a *loved one*? If this is true, where the heck have we gone wrong?

Those handhelds, which were supposed to speed up our work and give us more free time, are actually multiplying our work and packing it with us wherever we go. With our handhelds in tow, we can carry our work—and our problems—in our purses or pockets, to interrupt us at the beach, the spa, or the supermarket—and even to break into bedroom activity. ("Oh, sorry, dear, it's probably the boss—I'll be right back.") Sure, an hour later . . . after the mood has worn off.

Yes, it's important to keep track of your business and be connected to your coworkers, clients, and leaders. Handhelds have made this easier, particularly for those who don't spend most of their time in the office. But this easy connectivity is making people increasingly less able to turn it off. While technology can help you become more productive, it also blurs the lines between work time and personal time. Is it more productive to have one foot in the working world and one foot on the homefront at the same time? I'm not so sure, since you won't do either one very well.

If you're always available via e-mail or phone, compliments of your handheld, are you truly focusing on your loved ones when you're allegedly off work? Can you let loose and play if you're always poised to answer the next text? Unless your connection to work means life or death, you can and *should* turn off and tune out when the workday is over. It's time to put the brakes on your devices and decide to be the master, not the servant.

On a Disneyland vacation with my family last year, I witnessed numerous people typing away on their handhelds while walking around the park, with their children tugging at their pants legs, asking to go see Cinderella. I was presenting a seminar recently, and one participant kept looking up to say, "Would you repeat your last statement?" She wasn't paying attention to me; she was checking her e-mail on her iPhone during class.

A new study released July 26, 2007, by AOL, in partnership with Opinion Research Corporation, revealed that more Americans are using portable devices to e-mail around the clock from virtually anywhere—even in the bathroom and at church. Even more dangerously, 53 percent of respondents admit to tapping away *while driving.* Other interesting statistics:

- 83 percent of e-mail users are checking while on vacation.
- 59 percent of those with portable devices are using them to check e-mail every time a new message arrives.
- 43 percent keep the device nearby when they're sleeping to listen for incoming e-mail.

- 15 percent describe themselves as addicted to e-mail. (Only 15 percent? Oh, that was 2007.)

How depressing. AOL was extolling this like a virtue, of course; that you can stay connected anywhere, anytime. That's a dangerous message. We're teaching people that in order to be productive and valuable, you have to be "always on," give up your private time, and check e-mail at all hours of the night. Portable devices are convenient when you're traveling for business, sitting on an airplane, riding in a taxi, driving as a passenger in a car with nothing better to do, breaking at a business conference to stay in touch with the office, waiting to pick up your kid from soccer, and so on. But be careful about throwing yourself upon the altar of e-mail addiction and sacrificing the quality of your life balance and time with your loved ones.

Can you turn off your device for two hours while having a nice dinner with a spouse without thinking about it constantly? How about during a movie? Would you get hives if your Black-Berry wasn't charged? Do you feel like the world is going to end if you were without it for a day? Only you know, intuitively, whether you have a problem. SuperCompetents can control themselves. So if you think it's bad now, just wait to see what happens in a couple years.

No Nosing in on Family Time

The best and worst things about handhelds are improved access to information and the ability to work from virtually anywhere. We've never been more connected. For you, this might mean traveling with your laptop, never being without your handheld, or sneaking off in the evenings to check your office e-mail.

While this gives us more flexibility than ever before, it also means your work is a whole lot more likely to put its nose where it doesn't belong: smack dab in the middle of personal or family time. Despite a common misconception to the contrary, this is *not* what the road to success looks like. It's more like the road to burnout.

If you never turn work off, then your mind is never able to reenergize. Our bodies and brains need down time. Bringing work home and being plugged in after hours should be the exception, not the rule. Do you need to be accessible at all hours (as in a surgeon or IT manager), or is that restriction of your own doing? Exercise a little discipline and control it, rather than letting it control you. If you can't do it, then you're addicted.

Call Your Doctor Immediately If You Develop Antisocial Tendencies

Sometimes it feels as though the more technology brings us together, the more it pushes us apart. E-mail, voicemail, and instant messaging are all great communication tools, but they'll never take the place of good old-fashioned personal contact. Just because it's easier to pick up your handheld and fire off a quick e-mail doesn't always mean it's appropriate to do so. If you're dealing with a sensitive or personal issue, take the time to schedule a meeting, walk down the hall, and see someone face-to-face. These days, the novelty of speaking in person can go a long way toward getting things done and building productive relationships.

Do Not Drive or Operate Heavy Machinery

Technology does *not* belong behind the wheel. If you know you won't be able to resist checking e-mail on your phone the moment it beeps, shut it until you get where you're going. Many salespeople have admitted to me they drive with their *knees* or *elbows* and respond to e-mails while driving down the interstate. Please, *please*, don't do this! I saw a video of a bus driver who did and smashed into the car in front of him. Texting while driving is an accident waiting to happen, and the lives you endanger aren't just your own. In Colorado, texting while driving is illegal, and many other states have or are considering similar legislation. Perfect.

Break the Addiction

Handhelds should be helpful. They shouldn't suck you in, and they shouldn't be used as an excuse to work when you should be doing something more important, like being with your family, or heaven forbid, driving. And if you find you prefer your phone to your significant other, might I suggest you get some professional help?

If you place too much focus on the tools of the trade, rather than the work itself, the addiction is nearly as bad as smoking. You need to break free, so you can focus on being productive.

SUMMARY: ATTENTION

Ten-hut!

SuperCompetent people don't have nifty time-stretching devices like the one Hermione uses in Harry Potter to cram in extra courses at Hogwarts. Nope, they have the same number of hours and minutes we do, but they simply use them more efficiently. They know how to pay Attention to their work—and nothing else—when it's necessary, so they can stop paying Attention when they need to devote time to other important parts of their lives.

It all boils down to time. Do you have time to check your social media accounts constantly, especially if they have nothing to do with work? Of course not, but doing so is tempting, particularly when it takes you away from more onerous tasks. Being constantly connected makes it even easier to lose track of what you're doing and encourages you to waste time enjoying yourself, your shiny technology, and social interaction.

Let's face it. There's a time for work and a time for fun, and most of the time, you can't do both effectively simultaneously (at least, not while accomplishing anything worthwhile). So change your approach and focus, focus, focus. Social media, handhelds, and e-mail are tools for the SuperCompetent; use them for their intended purposes, instead of letting the entertainment factor get out of hand in the workplace.

And don't let the utility of these devices trick you into trying to do too much at once, either. Just because it's easy to communicate via e-mail and social media and get more work through your contacts doesn't mean that you should. You're only human; you can only do so much.

Go to www.TheProductivityPro.com/Attention to receive bonus material, the SuperCompetent Key 3 assessment questions, a summary, and the action-planning worksheet in Microsoft Word format. Get additional resources, audios, videos, and more at www.SuperCompetentBook.com.

ACTION PLANNING WORKSHEET: ATTENTION

11. I don't read each e-mail when it arrives; I'm able to stay focused on my work.
    What came to mind when I read this?

    _____
    _____
    _____
    _____

    What is my action plan for improvement?

    _____
    _____
    _____
    _____

12. I leave distractions for my downtime.
    What came to mind when I read this?

    _____
    _____
    _____
    _____

    What is my action plan for improvement?

    _____
    _____
    _____
    _____

13. I can do only one thing at a time, so I limit my
    multitasking to maximize my productivity.
    What came to mind when I read this?

    _____

    _____

    _____

    _____

    What is my action plan for improvement?

    _____

    _____

    _____

    _____

14. I don't allow socializing to overwhelm my productivity,
    whether online or in real life.
    What came to mind when I read this?

    _____

    _____

    _____

    _____

    What is my action plan for improvement?

    _____

    _____

    _____

    _____

15. I know technology and my handheld are tools to help me
    be more productive—no addiction here.
    What came to mind when I read this?

    _____

    _____

    _____

    _____

    What is my action plan for improvement?

    _____

    _____

    _____

    _____

PART 4

SuperCompetent Key 4: Accessibility

SuperCompetent people can quickly find the information they need.

ACCESSIBILITY is the ability to organize the inputs and outputs in your life.

This key gives you the systems you need to locate data contained in any medium: paper, e-mail, phone calls, contacts, Internet, and so on.

When I was in college in the mid-80s, I attended my first time-management course. The instructor told us to write down our schedules for the entire day, including the specific time we would work on each task. I dutifully wrote up-to-the-minute agendas, detailing what I would complete: "From 8:00 to 8:30, I'll do this . . . from 8:30 to 9:10, I'll do this . . ."

Back then, I could pretty much keep up with it, and the day usually went as planned. When something unexpected arose, it was fairly easy to adjust my plan. Then things started to change: Technology exploded, voicemail, e-mail, and the Internet entered the scene, and the productivity game was forever altered. If you attempted nowadays to write out every minute of your day, how long would your schedule last? It would probably blow up in the first five minutes. You could probably spend more time revising the plan than simply doing your work!

Indeed, it has become harder to be productive, for all these reasons:

- We're busier than ever before—because we have more to do, with fewer resources, and less time to do it in.
- We're more disorganized than ever before, because we receive information from multiple sources and have more data to track and organize.
- We're constantly communicating with more people, more quickly, through more media, so we have more conversations and history to recall.

Being productive today requires many different competencies—one of which is being organized. If you excel in this competency, you likely have systems, rather than piles of paper and piles of files. If you're organized, you can find what you want when you want it—in 30 seconds or less. Being organized means controlling the paper, e-mail, reading material, and inputs into and out of your office and life. Organization is your ability to sort, filter, and process all types of information effectively. It's how tidy your office (and home) looks, inside and out. It's how in control you look and feel, inside and out. Being organized will give you more control over your life and time. SuperCompetents find the time and the self-control to achieve organization through proper systems.

CHAPTER 16

I Know I Have a System Around Here Somewhere . . .

SUPERCOMPETENT Hero Thinking:	I've created the perfect time-management system for my personality, job environment, and work situation.
SIMPLY COMPETENT Zero Thinking:	I don't have any *time* to develop systems! I'm overwhelmed as it is!

Organizing your life is complicated by the fact that different people use different systems and have different personalities. We all face diverse work situations and environments, each of which is conducive to a variety of organizational approaches. There's no one-size-fits-all or one correct method of organizing. Some of it depends upon your preferences, and some depends upon your job. Some of it depends upon whether you travel or on the availability of technology. So whether you use paper-based or electronic systems—or some hybrid of the two—your ability to coordinate everything will depend upon several factors.

An Organizational Systems Assessment

Not sure where you lie on the paper/electronic continuum? Start by taking this assessment to determine where your preferences lie.

Answer Yes or No: Circle the corresponding letter	Yes	No
1. Do you work primarily at a fixed-office desk?	A	B
2. Are you constantly on the go?	B	A
3. Do you print your e-mail?	A	B
4. Do you enjoy using calendaring software on your computer?	B	A
5. Do you take a lot of notes in meetings and on the phone?	A	B
6. Do you need a relatively inexpensive time-management system?	A	B
7. Do you need the ability to immediately glance at your complete monthly calendar?	A	B
8. Do you track your friends' and relatives' names, addresses, and phone numbers on a computer?	B	A
9. Does your work require quick access to thousands of names, phone numbers, and addresses?	B	A
10. Do you need to be able to access your e-mail while traveling?	B	A
11. Do you travel infrequently?	A	B
12. Does double entry (writing then typing) feel like a waste of time?	A	B
13. Are you comfortable having no backup system, if you lose it?	A	B
14. Do you dislike rewriting to-do lists?	B	A
15. Do you run out of room to write to-do lists?	B	A
16. Do you carry papers around with you to meetings?	A	B

	Yes	No
17. Do you want to carry something small and lightweight?	B	A
18. Do you carry around confidential information?	B	A

Scoring:
Number of A responses: _____
Number of B responses: _____

More "A" responses indicates a preference for paper-based systems, whereas more "B" responses imply that you prefer—or need—more electronic or software based systems. If you were tied 9–9, or had a close score like 8–10 or 10–8, you tend to employ hybrid-based systems, or combinations of both paper and electronic methods.

There's no one right way to organize. You need to do what feels natural, easy, and most efficient for you. I know several people who felt pressured to get a handheld because everyone else was getting one. One woman never took hers out of the box. One fellow tried it and hated being "tethered to it," so it became a big paperweight on his desk. One seminar attendee reported she wasn't nearly as organized with her handheld. She now had sticky notes everywhere because it hurt her thumbs to type into it, so she reverted back to her paper planner system. But I know other people who have five different sizes and brands of paper planners—all collecting dusk on their bookshelves.

Technologies like smart phones, web-based applications, desktop applications, and PDAs have given us so many options when it comes to keeping track of what we need to do. But figuring out the best system for you can be a real challenge (and a frustrating one).

Primarily, it's critical to customize your system to your needs. Perhaps you have to use electronic calendaring software at your workplace to allow others to check your schedule and plan meetings, but you're truly a paper person at your core. Go ahead and use the software if you must, but copy meetings to your paper calendar if you prefer to carry it with you. You might argue that this is double entry, but trying to force yourself to use something you hate makes you not use it at all, I'd absolutely recommend double entry. And it's not right for everyone; you should only worry about what's right for *you*.

Interestingly enough, even with all the technology out there, a good amount of informal research (mine and others') still shows when push comes to shove, most people still fall back on good old-fashioned paper. In fact, a recent lifehack.org survey (www .lifehack.org/articles/lifehack/where-do-you-keep-your-todo-list .html) shows that not only do most people use a paper to-do list, but paper is more than twice as popular as any other method listed. I asked in an informal survey I conducted via LinkedIn, "When you think of something you need to do, what do you usually do?" More than half (58 percent) said they write it down somewhere.

Why? Because we're human. Life doesn't always happen when you're sitting in front of your computer. We sit in meetings. We leave the office and go home. We travel. No matter how attached we are to our iPhones and BlackBerries—and no matter how sophisticated the technology becomes—most people simply don't like making lists or taking notes while squinting at a tiny screen or getting thumb cramps trying to punch in line after line of text (which is why I created The Productivity Pro® planner for the handheld user by Day-Timer at www.daytimer.com/ productivity). Though handhelds are great for portability and storing reference information, they're just not configured for extensive note taking. Many handheld users end up being the most disorganized and messy of us all. Without a paper planner, the inevitable to-do lists and reminders end up scattered all over the place on sticky notes and little scraps of paper. Lack of a home for it all lets these notes become disorganized, lost, and useless.

So what's the solution? Let's look at some of the most popular approaches to organizing and see if we can find a solution that's uniquely fitted to you.

Paper Planners

Interestingly, people who use paper planners *exclusively* are often the best organized of us all. Such tools allow you to have your system available at all times, combine your personal and professional lives, get an instant view of your schedule, and keep manageable to-do lists. I meet countless people in my seminars who tell me how they abandoned their trusty paper systems in search of paperless PDA methods—just to become so disorganized they reverted back to paper.

However, for all the advantages, there are challenges with using strictly paper:

- It's often impractical to keep track of hundreds of contacts on paper.
- Other workers in your organization can't check your availability if your current calendar isn't reflected.
- Your assistant can't schedule appointments for you easily without worry of double booking.
- You can't access your e-mail from the road via a paper planner.

Desktop Software

Perhaps you could use desktop computer software, such as Outlook, Lotus, or GroupWise. This allows you to manage your contacts, calendar, and to-do lists in one place without working with a pocket-sized interface.

In fact, desktop software is absolutely perfect, assuming you never, ever leave your desk. But you *do* have to go home. And then, when you think of something you need to do at work, you have to make a note. And the scrapping begins. You probably have meetings. If someone says, "Let's meet again next Thursday. What's your schedule?" Your very unprofessional response is, "Uh, I don't know. It's on my calendar back at my desk." How can you expect someone to trust you to manage an important project if you can't control your own schedule?

Business and life have a tendency to happen on their own terms. Therefore, it's important to have a system in place for gathering things like notes, appointments, and contact information—at least until you get back to your desk. You should have a paper system to supplement whatever you're doing electronically. You could use a spiral notebook, though it can soon become disorganized because of the rigid binding. Notes, to-do lists, phone numbers, and random information are all mixed together, forcing you to go back and reread, rewrite, and re-organize.

You could also print your Outlook calendars, carry them around with you, handwrite updates, and periodically enter the data and reprint. Or you could sync to a handheld. I personally hate tapping on the tiny screen all the time. Don't get me wrong—I love my handheld—but mostly for e-mail, texting, phone calls, and contact management. I prefer to see a big-picture view of my schedule and things to do on my trusty paper system, The Productivity Pro® planner by Day-Timer (www.daytimer .com/productivity). I just don't feel creative when I'm not putting pen to paper, and a centralized system beats scraps of paper every time!

Web-Based Applications

As it becomes easier and easier to find an Internet connection when you need one (or if you happen to have an air card), Web-based applications, such as Gmail, can be a great organizational tool. Whether you use the Web simply to access your calendar or are set up to remotely access your entire PC, it's nice to be able to get what you need from any computer with an Internet connection.

Especially if you travel often, using Web-based software comes in handy where traditional desktop software might break down. You don't need to get to *your* computer; you just need to get to *a* computer. However, Web-based software has the same problem as desktop software—it isn't always going to be at your fingertips. As with a desktop application, you might still need a paper supplement.

If different people are maintaining separate Outlook calendars, it might make sense to share and synchronize them with groupware programs such as www.familyscheduleronline.com, which allows family members to access the family calendar from any Internet connection. Similarly, ShareCalendar (www.4team.biz) sends your family members updated Calendar items (appointments, meetings, events) by regular e-mail. It lets you update and manage all your shared Calendar folders offline or using any Internet connection. Or remember www.doodle.com to offer date and time options to people who don't work for the same company.

Handheld Devices Are Tying My Hands

When I refer to *handheld*, I basically mean anything small enough to fit in your pocket—a PDA, Windows Mobile device, Treo, BlackBerry, iPhone, Droid, smart phone, whatever. When handhelds started catching on, many were probably thinking our organization problems were solved. After all, we could finally have the best of both worlds: technology and portability.

Unfortunately, most of us quickly found no matter how sophisticated an electronic device could become, it still didn't quite cut it for organization. Most people grab pencil and paper when they think of something to do and take notes in meetings by hand. The task list isn't always user friendly on a handheld, because you have to rummage through your purse, power it on, find the application, and tap out your thoughts. Even if you understand categories well enough and can sort your list, the devices often max out at 15 categories. And nobody wants to scribble with a stylus or furiously thumb-type through a meeting or conversation. (I gave myself a painful condition called BlackBerry Thumb from attempting it and actually had to wear a wrist brace for three weeks!) Even if you do get all the information entered properly, tiny navigation screens and even tinier font sizes just don't quite cut it.

Handheld devices are great when you need to enter a new contact's information on the fly or check to see if your schedule is open two Thursdays from now. However, they still can't do the job of simple pen and paper when it comes to writing notes and creating lists. They are good for *reference* but not for *capture*.

The Solution—a Hybrid Method!

It's getting progressively harder to find people who don't use some form of electronic organizing tool, yet even the most tech-savvy tend to fall back on paper for some tasks. If you're listening to a voicemail on your phone, what are you doing? Writing down the message. Bingo—you need a paper planner. When you're talking to the Hertz customer-service agent on the phone, and he asks for your Gold number, what are you doing? Trying not to hang up on the person while you mumble, "Uh, hang on, it's in my . . . phone." You need a paper planner. You're sitting in a meeting talking with your biggest client. What are you doing? Typing notes with your thumbs while attempting to listen? I doubt it. Again, you need a paper planner—one place that consolidates your lists, reference information, and notes.

I became so frustrated watching people struggle to find an effective way to use their handhelds in the real world that I teamed up with Day-Timer to create a paper system specifically designed for users of handheld organizers (although it works just as well for people who don't have one). The Productivity Pro® planner by Day-Timer has monthly calendar tabs but no time slots on the daily pages (the detailed information in your calendar is probably kept in Outlook or your handheld). This provides a large, easy-to-manage writing space for your notes, lists, and those pesky to-dos that always seem to be slipping through the cracks otherwise. It also has tools to help with things like long-range planning and on-going lists—things that don't always have an intuitive home within electronic organizers. Incidentally, I designed The Productivity Pro® planner with rings, so the pages could be moved around easily. (Visit www.daytimer.com/laurastack or www.daytimer.com/productivity to check it out!)

Find a System That Works for You

Each of us has a different way of organizing things, based on an individual's knowledge, personality, and background. Some of us function best by focusing strictly on paper methods; others prefer electronic; and for many of us, the best method combines elements of the two. If you're uncertain where you fall on this continuum—or whether the system you're using would be better replaced with another—try a different method for at least a few weeks to see how it goes. At the worst, it'll help you take some steps in the right direction.

Find a good system—one that works for *you* and keeps you consistently productive. Once you get that settled, you won't have to waste time with something that doesn't work. This will help other things fall into place, and you can use the time you've saved to sit down and figure out how to be even more productive; or better yet, you can go home early and enjoy life.

CHAPTER 17

Um, What Was I Supposed to Do Today?

SUPERCOMPETENT Hero Thinking:	I know exactly where I'm supposed to be and exactly what I should be working on at all times.
SIMPLY COMPETENT Zero Thinking:	Are you kidding me? When am I supposed to find time to organize my schedule?

SuperCompetents know what they should be doing and where they should be at any given time. They have highly organized calendars and to-do lists and know exactly what they should be working on during periods of discretionary time. They break projects down into manageable pieces, so their short-term actions translate into long-term success.

Things to Do

To-do lists are necessary for keeping track of action items: Things that we must do at some point but don't necessarily have to be done at a specified time (as a meeting on your calendar does).

To-do lists let you write something down so you *can* forget it, which allows your brain to be less cluttered. For example, if you needed a few items at the grocery store, you could make a list, run in, and grab just the items you need. Or you could walk up and down each aisle, looking at every product, hoping your eye would catch something and trigger your memory. If you get the shopping done a half hour earlier by using the list, you could be spending your time doing more important things.

How do you handle it when you think of something you need to do? Do you simply add it to a list? Make a new task in Outlook? Write it on a sticky note? Put it in your spiral notebook? Many methods for tracking action items are inefficient and disorganized, especially if you're trying to figure out what to do *this very minute* with a list of 87 things in front of you. How do you know if you're making good choices? To effectively organize your time, you need several different types of lists.

Daily to-do list. Essentially your daily plan or marching orders, this list captures everything you truly intend to get done today. It's *not* an ongoing list of everything you need to do—as in the master to-do list. Unlike the master to-do list, I only have one daily to-do list. I integrate my personal and professional lives into a single list because the lines are often blurred (some personal items can only be done on a lunch hour or breaks between the hours of 9:00 to 5:00). A daily to-do list is the first thing you see in the morning and the last thing you see before leaving the office. It keeps you focused and on-target throughout the day.

Master to-do list. This is a running list of *everything* you need or want to do. Think of it as your memory list; you need one for work and one for personal items. Every time you think of something you need to do, capture it on your master to-do list. This tool keeps your daily to-do list from having 87 items on it. For example, my master list currently contains "Replace border in James' bedroom" and "Investigate new wireless earpiece microphone options." A master to-do list is an ongoing list to keep track of things you might want to do someday that aren't ready to move to your daily to-do list.

When composing this list, think about:

- Calls you need to make
- Letters that need to be sent
- Errands you need to run
- Furniture to be bought or cleaned
- Purchases
- Vacations or travel

- New projects you want to start
- Files and records
- Equipment to be bought or repaired
- Financial matters
- Feedback to give or get

- Meetings to schedule or attend
- Waiting for work from others
- Think about your desk organization
- Closet
- Chores or living space

- Appliances
- Yard work/ outdoors
- Health/doctor
- Exercise
- Books to read
- Pets
- Car
- Birthdays
- Items borrowed—to return or get back
- Supplies

Organizing Options for Daily and Master To-Do Lists

1. *Paper.* I use a two-page-per-day option for my daily to-do list. On the left, I write people I need to contact and errands I need to run. On the right, I write things I need to do. I file my master to-do list behind the letter "M" in my A–Z tabs. When I think of something I need to do, I ask myself when it will be done. If it's that day (or within the month of daily pages I keep in my planner), I write it on a daily page. If I don't have a deadline or it's beyond the current month, I write it on my master list.

2. *Electronic Methods.* Microsoft Outlook calls to-do items Tasks (same thing). A task is a personal or work-related action item you want to track until it's completed. A task can occur once or repeatedly, and a recurring task can repeat at regular intervals or based on the date you mark it completed. For example, you might want to send a status report to your manager on the last Friday of every month or get a haircut when one month has passed since your last haircut.

To make a system purely electronic, you'd sync your software with your handheld device, so you can access your tasks wherever you are. This works particularly well for people who travel a lot and can't access their desktops.

3. *Hybrid Methods.* Some people keep track of what they need to do in a software package, but they're rarely at their computers to refer to it. They print their to-do list and carry it around, rather than syncing to a handheld device. Because this is an electronic/paper combination system, it is considered a hybrid method.

Still others create their own forms using word processing or spreadsheet software. They track their lists electronically, and then they print them out and carry them around for reference and manual updates. Some three-hole punch the paper and keep them in a three-ring binder. Remember: It doesn't have to be expensive!

Category Lists. Category lists are another type of list with groups of related reminder items. If your friend told you about a great restaurant she visited, would you be able to remember the name four months later? If your dad rented a movie he highly recommends, will you be able to recall the name the next time you're wandering the video store aisles? What if it's your wife's birthday, but you absolutely cannot remember the perfect gift you thought of two months ago? Some information isn't necessarily actionable: It's based on recall. Reminders aren't necessarily things you need to track on your to-do list; you don't know when you'll do them, since you're not sure when you'll need the information again. You also need reminders about important events such as birthdays or anniversaries. Organizing this type of item can be confusing, but again, it involves a simple solution: category lists.

Here are some examples of the category lists I currently track:

- Article ideas for my newsletter
- Blog topics
- Birthdays and anniversaries
- Books to read (I may or may not eventually purchase or get from the library.)

- Bus stop info
- Combination locks (so I can take the sticker off)
- Errands to run
- Gift ideas (cool things to buy for birthdays and holidays)
- Groceries to buy (even though "go to grocery store" may be an item on my daily to-do list, this list contains the individual items I need to remember to buy)
- Honey-do's (a list of things I need to remember to ask my husband to do at some point)
- Personal data (where I track Social Security numbers, driver's license number, clothes sizes, blood types, and so on. You never know!)
- Projects
- Restaurants
- Shopping list (a list of things I need to remember to get when I'm running errands)
- Soccer (team roster, practice and game date reference)
- Speech ideas
- Vacation ideas
- Videos to rent
- Wines to try
- Wish list

Any list your brain can imagine, you can and should track!

Organizing Options for Category Lists

Here are some different ways to organize your category lists:

1. *Paper.* If you use a paper planner, you can file category lists behind the A–Z tabs. Although these tabs are normally used for addresses and phone numbers (as mine are), they also work as a paper filing system. I use lined pages the size of my planner and write the name of the list across the top—Gifts, Shopping, Errands, Projects—and file it behind the letter of the list. For example, I keep my master task list under M, my question list for my mentor Dianna Booher behind B, and the staff phone directory of the National Speakers Association behind N. You can also track subordinates, key coworkers, clients, your boss,

spouse, children, and so on this way. As you think of topics you need to discuss with others but don't have time to do immediately, simply make a note in those logs. When you have several items saved up, you can call to schedule an appointment to review your thoughts. Or, you can refer to this section in a scheduled weekly or biweekly meeting with subordinates.

If you don't have a planner, you could simply use the same three-ring binder you're using for your calendar and to-do templates, add A–Z dividers (you can purchase them at any office supply store), use loose-leaf paper, and file the pages behind the corresponding letter. Some people just keep a spiral notebook with a different list on each page, skipping a few pages in between to allow for growth and rewrites.

2. *Electronic.* If you're an electronic person, you have several options. Some people prefer to use their calendaring and task software and keep a running task or to-do for each category. Some people prefer Excel spreadsheets or Word documents. Many Outlook users have discovered the power of Notes (in the BlackBerry, these are under Memo Pad). It's a powerful, underutilized feature, which is perfect for category lists.

Notes are the electronic equivalent of paper sticky notes. Use them to track lists of items, jot down things to remember to discuss with a direct report, keep track of ideas for an upcoming meeting, gather clippings from the web, and take notes during a meeting. You can leave Notes open on the screen while you work, which is especially convenient when you're using the tool for storing bits of information you may need later, such as directions or text you want to reuse in other items or documents.

To be completely electronic, you would sync your handheld to your software and have your category lists at your fingertips wherever you are. Other Internet sites offer e-mail and cell phone electronic reminder systems for common events such as birthdays, anniversaries, and home maintenance, such as www.birthdayreminders.com, www.dates2remember.com, www.happybirthday.com, and www.bigdates.com.

3. *Hybrid Methods.* Perhaps you don't have a handheld but still want to use Outlook Notes for your Category lists. If you use both a paper planner and Outlook as I do, you could simply

print your electronic Notes on the same size paper as your planner and file them behind your A–Z tabs.

Appointments and Meetings

Keeping your calendar straight is a huge endeavor. With so many choices and technologies, it can be difficult to know what's best. Paper planner or BlackBerry? Printed calendar from your computer or a diary? Wall calendar or Internet solution?

Making sure your schedule reflects your business, personal, and family lives is a big key to success. Have you ever been in a meeting where your colleagues ask when everyone can meet next, and you have to respond, "I don't know," because you don't have an up-to-date calendar? Have you ever been on the phone at home talking to a friend who wants to have lunch on Tuesday, and you vaguely remember a commitment but don't know for sure, because you can't check your work calendar from home? If you don't have a system containing your entire life in one, easy-to-use tool, you'll inevitably face conflicts.

1. *Paper Methods.* Many people use paper methods to keep track of their schedules, which appears to be a trend continuing into the foreseeable future. These paper methods come in a variety of forms.
   - *Agendas.* A multitude of paper calendars—each designed to fit different needs—are widely available. A month-at-a-glance may be all you require if you have a couple of meetings or appointments per day. A week-at-a-glance is helpful if you have many meetings and need more room to write notes, comments, and details (think nail salons, hair stylists, and counselors). If you think the boxes on a monthly calendar are too small, you may want to use a weekly calendar. A day-at-a-glance is helpful if you like to use your calendar as a combination appointment tracker and to-do list.
   - *Planning Systems.* Other systems offer an expanded planning system, often with fancy leather covers, customized inserts, and additional information tracking. They provide one- or two-page-per-day systems, which are perfect if you want to keep daily appointments, your to-do list, meeting directions,

and notes all in one place. For people who don't have a hand-held, the Productivity Pro® planner by Day-Timer (www .daytimer.com/productivity) also allows you to print your Outlook calendar on special print-your-own pages and insert them into your planner.

- *Templates*. An alternative to purchasing more expensive systems is to create your own customized calendar templates on your computer. Use a word processing program to design a blank template, make copies of it, write in the days and months, three-hole-punch it, and keep it in a three-ring binder.

- *Wall Calendars*. Some families prefer a large, paper wall calendar to track their various schedules and commitments. Designate one place in your home to hang the family calendar—this will be command central for your family. Assign each person a corresponding pen color or colored dot sticker to record appointments on the family calendar, which is especially critical if the appointment affects more than one person. If your child needs a ride, for example, that time is marked on the family calendar in that child's color (with the pen or dot). If you're keeping a separate work calendar, make sure to update it with any information from the family calendar that might influence your business life. This is an important point. If you don't write personal activities or children's school events on your work calendar as well, you *will* have conflicts.

2. *Electronic Methods*. Perhaps paper methods aren't for you. I've had people look at my Day-Timer binder (I use the Day-Timer portable size) and groan, "Yuck, I could never carry one of those big things around!" (I personally think it's quite small.) So maybe you'd be better off experimenting with an electronic method.

   - *Software*. At home, computer programs like Microsoft's trusty $39.95 Works (version 9) gives you all the features you need for a calendar without the triple-digit price of its bigger sibling, Microsoft Office. One noteworthy feature is its ability to let up to four family members create and merge their own color-coded calendars to keep everyone up to speed. Of course, the most common electronic calendaring applications are the more robust versions used by corporations to schedule meetings: Outlook, GroupWise, and Lotus Notes (there are other platforms, of course, but these are the most common). I've focused mostly on Outlook in this book, because it's used by the majority of corporations. If you have to keep your work schedule on an electronic calendar because of workplace policy, you could also create a separate calendar for your personal life and view them side by side. Your main work calendar is the only one that can be viewed by those sharing your calendar, but you can still see your personal commitments without blocking out time on your work calendar.

- *Handheld.* To keep it handy, most electronic calendar users then sync their software to their handheld device. There are many, many options for handheld devices; many depend on which service provider you use. Using calendaring software with a handheld is the ultimate electronic option. However, it's not for everyone!

3. *Hybrid Methods.* Enter combination methods. If you use a daily planner for your work activities and a wall calendar at home for your family plans, record every family event that affects your personal time in your planner. Since the line between work and home is often blurred these days, it's critical to have the ability to see your entire schedule at one time. You could carry your paper calendar or planner back and forth from work and home. Or you could print your work calendar on paper, carry it home in your briefcase, update it by hand with personal information as necessary, then update your work calendar (checking the Private box if you wish) and reprint it at work about once a week.

Some might worry about the inefficiency of this double entry. Perhaps you have to use electronic calendaring software at your workplace to allow others to check your schedule and plan meetings. Or perhaps you haven't been authorized a BlackBerry because your job description isn't high enough (I'd argue a business case for an exception). Note your commitments there if you must, but copy them as well to your paper calendar.

This is actually what I do myself. I use my Day-Timer to track my schedule and to-dos. If I want more detail, it's on my Windows Mobile phone. My handheld allows me to handle e-mail on the go, but I don't use it to write to-do lists. I also use Outlook and then sync it to my handheld, but I dislike tapping the screen with the little stylus. It takes longer to select the little box for each day and try to see my month than it does to open my paper planner. I actually *enjoy* writing, and I like seeing all my appointments for the month. So I continue to use hybrid methods, even though I have the knowledge and technology to go completely paperless. The choice is up to you!

My situation requires that multiple people be aware of my travel activities, including my employees, husband, family, agents, and clients. Because they all work virtually in different locations, our solution to this particular dilemma is a Web-based calendar. Many different versions are available on the Internet; we use one specifically designed for professional speakers and meeting professionals at www.eSpeakers.com. Each day, these individuals can pull up my schedule on the calendar or web site (www.theproductivitypro.com/m_info_calendar.htm) and know exactly where I am and how to get a hold of me. I receive an e-mail when a staff member schedules a speaking engagement for me, so I can update my paper planner calendar accordingly.

I hope this section allows you to see the myriad organizing options for your calendar. Your job now is to pick one method, implement it, and consistently apply it. You don't want to do different things at different times; you'll just confuse yourself about what you did with an item. If, after several weeks of attempting to implement a particular method, it isn't flowing for you, choose a different alternative and try again.

Prime Your Productivity

You're never going to be productive until you're able to manage your time efficiently. We've discussed various methods—paper, electronic, and hybrid—of keeping your to-do lists and calendar organized. For the purpose of scheduling, these approaches apply primarily to appointments, to-do lists, and meetings. Hopefully this chapter has made it easier to apply all three organizational methods to those topics and will help you get started on your quest to prime your productivity.

CHAPTER 18

You're the Boss,
Not Your Inbox!

SUPERCOMPETENT Hero Thinking:	My e-mail is organized, and my inbox is regularly emptied.
SIMPLY COMPETENT Zero Thinking:	I have 20,000 messages in my inbox; it's just a giant filing cabinet.

My first (real) corporate job was with TRW Defense Systems in Colorado Springs, CO. I can still remember my co-workers "oooohhhing" and "ahhhhhing" over the brand-new fax machine in the department. (Remember those grease-paper rolls?) Even then, I can recall thinking, "This can't be a good idea." When we put documents in the regular mail, the turnaround time was at least a week. Then the fax machine came along . . . and our customers got used to instant gratification. Then came voicemail, then the cell phone, the pager, and then everything hit the fan when e-mail exploded on the scene.

How many hours do you spend wading around in your e-mail inbox each day? E-mail isn't a toy—it's a tool—a means of making yourself more productive. If you let yourself be chained down by your e-mail instead of letting it help set you free, you're never likely to get much done. Here are my top 10 best practices to take advantage of your e-mail without letting it take advantage of you.

As a Microsoft Certified Application Specialist in Outlook, I will give the instructions in Outlook 2007. If you're using Outlook 2003 or a different e-mail platform such as Lotus or GroupWise, the principle remains the same, but the commands may vary slightly.

Best Practices for E-mail Organization

To effectively organize your e-mail, implement the following best practices:

1. *The Inbox is not a to-do list*. Pull the action from the e-mail and move it to the correct location. Do *not* simply flag the e-mail, which simply leaves it in the inbox.
    a. Right–click on the e-mail.
    b. Select "Move to Folder" from the shortcut menu.
    c. Select Tasks from the list if it's a to-do item or select Calendar if it has a specific time.
    d. Click OK.
    e. This will activate a task properties window.
    f. Update all of the information accordingly. Use the "Start Date" to indicate when you want the task to appear on your To-Do bar.
    g. Click the "Save and Close" button.
    h. Make sure your TaskPad (2003) or To-Do bar (2007) sorts by Start Date, not Due Date.

    If you'd rather work with a paper copy, print any e-mail that requires future work or follow up and file it in a paper tickler file with 43 hanging folders: 1–31 for the days of the month and 12 for the months. Then create a personal e-mail folder called @Tickler and drag the e-mail requiring follow up. When the paper copy (trigger) comes up in your tickler file, you know the original is in your @Tickler folder, which will save you from retyping the e-mail message when you respond to it.

2. *Use Sent Items for "filing" and searches*. If you are always the last to respond to an e-mail—even just to say, "Thank you for the

information. I appreciate your time and look forward to seeing you next week," and so forth—then you can use your Sent Items for searches by person, subject, date, and so on, rather than filing them in personal folders.

3. *File e-mail in your existing folder system.* You already have a folder system on your hard drive or a shared drive. Rather than keeping a different list of personal folders in your Outlook, save e-mails in your existing folders to keep reference items together. Just as you would save a Word document or PowerPoint show, you can save e-mail as a file. While viewing the e-mail:
   a. Under the File menu, select Save As.
   b. Navigate to the correct folder on your hard or shared drive.
   c. Change the file name, if desired.
   d. In the Save as Type drop-down menu, select Outlook Message Format (*.msg).
   e. Click Save.
   f. When you double-click the Outlook icon, the e-mail will open within your Outlook software, just as if it were in the inbox.

4. *Reuse your e-mails.* Create signatures to use as letter templates. Expand your definition of a "signature" to be a reply or letter that you reuse often:
   a. On the Tools menu, click Options.
   b. Click the Mail Format tab.
   c. Select Signatures.
   d. Click "New."
   e. Type a name for your new template.
   f. Choose "Start with a blank template."
   g. Click Next.
   h. Copy/paste or type your letter or response.
   i. Click Finish.
   j. To use your signature, reply to the e-mail or start an e-mail as you normally would.
   k. On the Insert menu, click Signatures (only if you don't use MS Word as your e-mail editor).
   l. Select the name of your new signature.

5. *Stop asking a group of people their opinion.* Instead, take a poll and auto-tally the results. Rather than asking 10 people a question

and getting 47 responses when someone uses "Reply to All," take a vote instead:

  a. Start an e-mail as usual.

  b. Click the Options tab. In 2007, under the Tracking group, select Use Voting Buttons.

  c. Click the drop-down arrow and select your choice. There are three choices displayed to you, so make sure to phrase your e-mail in a way that will allow people to answer as you've selected.

  d. Or select Custom, and you can type in your own choices if you follow the pattern of the suggested choices (separate your options with a semicolon). For example, if you want people to vote on a choice of food for a dinner, include choices such as Burgers; Pizza; Beer; Chicken. You may include as many items as you'd like.

  e. The choices appear in the text box.

  f. Click close and send the e-mail.

  g. When recipients receive the e-mail, they will click the Vote drop-down menu in the Respond group. You might want to point this out in your message.

  h. When responses start arriving, you'll see each person's response in the subject and the top line of the e-mail. The text of the e-mail will also include any other message the recipient typed before sending the response.

  i. To get a full tally of the vote, find the original message you e-mailed in your Sent Items. It will be marked with a small letter *i* for interactive.

  j. Open the e-mail.

  k. Click the Tracking tab, where you will find a list of all recipients and their individual responses. The banner at the top of the message also shows the cumulative total of all votes.

6. *Don't assume that Sent means Done.* Set reminders. If you send someone an e-mail and are worried they won't reply or want to remind them about a deadline:

  a. Immediately after sending the original e-mail, go to your Sent Items (it will be the first entry in the list if sorting by the Sent field).

  b. Drag the e-mail to Tasks and drop.

    c. A new Task will automatically open up, with a copy of your e-mail in the text portion of the message.

    d. Do not set a Start Date or Due Date. This isn't actually a to-do.

    e. Instead, click the Reminder box and set a day and time. (I always set my reminders for 9:00 AM, so I get all of them in one box at one time.)

7. *Automate manual actions.* Use Outlook's Rules; they help you manage your e-mail messages by performing actions on messages that match a specific set of conditions. After you create a rule, Outlook applies it when a message arrives in your Inbox or when you send a message. Spend some time playing with the Rules Wizard to explore all the cool things you can do, such as forwarding to a list, automatically deleting mail from certain people, printing, moving messages where you're cc'd into a specified folder, or moving messages with certain words in the subject field to a folder.

    a. On the Tools menu, click Rules and Alerts.

    b. Click New Rule.

    c. Make sure the "Start creating a rule from a template" button is selected.

    d. Follow the Wizard.

8. *Don't allow yourself to become distracted by every e-mail.* Remove global alerts and create custom alerts for important people.

    a. Select Tools, Options.

    b. Click E-mail Options.

    c. Click Advanced E-mail Options.

    d. Uncheck all the boxes under "When new items arrive in my Inbox."

    e. Click OK.

    f. Now, create a rule to play a sound for "important" people.

    g. Right-click on an e-mail in the Inbox or Deleted Items FROM a person for whom you'd like to create a rule.

    h. Select "Create Rule."

    i. Click the "From (person's name)" box and "Play a selected sound" box.

    j. If you click "Advanced Options," you will see a lot of other features.

9. *Create a personalized menu with your favorite commands.*

    a. Right-click in any toolbar.

b. Select Customize.

c. The Customize dialog box will appear.

d. Click the Commands tab.

e. Under the Categorize list, select New Menu at the bottom of the list.

f. Drag the arrow (the New Menu icon) to the Menu bar where you want it located.

g. Right-click on the New Menu and click on Name and type in the desired name.

h. Click on your new menu to expand it. You'll see a blank box.

i. From the still-open Customize dialog box, click the Categories that contain your favorite menu options and drag as many as you want up to your new menu. Mix and match from any of the choices.

j. Click Close and test your new menu!

10. *Don't manually clean your mailbox.* Run AutoArchive.

a. Select Tools menu, Options

b. Click the "Other" tab.

c. Click AutoArchive.

d. Fill in the boxes as appropriate for how often you want to archive to your hard drive (I use 14 days). If you want a prompt (I like this option, since it can take a while to archive and can tie up your computer); delete expired items; Archive—DON'T delete—old items; show archive folder in folder list, clean out items older than (x) months; specify where on the hard drive you would like your archive folder to reside.

e. Click "Apply these settings to all folders now."

f. Click OK.

g. Your new Archive folders are now added to the bottom of your folder list.

Changes in Latitude, Changes in Attitude

If you let yourself be chained down by your technology instead of letting it help set you free, you're likely to never get much done. E-mail was invented in the first place to help you get more things done. Most of the e-mail you get is going to be spam or something equally unimportant. After all, how many times do you have to read that a duck's quack doesn't echo, or Bill Gates will give you money if you help him test his e-mail program? (Both are false, by the way.)

CHAPTER 19

We Don't Need No Steenking Rolodexes!

SUPERCOMPETENT Hero Thinking:	I keep careful track of my contacts and my communications with them; I can tell you what was said in a meeting a year ago.
SIMPLY COMPETENT Zero Thinking:	I've got that person's e-mail and phone number around here somewhere. If I hunt for it, I'm sure I can find it.

I had a manager in the mid-80s who had three huge Rolodexes on his desk to house his collection of business cards. I still remember watching him proudly flip through the thousands of cards, hunting for the right one that could help you solve your problem or answer a question. However, if he couldn't remember his contact's name or company, it often took him a long time to find that person.

Technology has made contact management easier in some ways, but the speed at which we now operate poses unique challenges:

- We communicate with more people than ever before.
- Technology provides more media with which we can communicate.

- The speed with which people expect you to respond to communication has likewise increased.
- Global markets have expanded, so we talk with people all over the world, most of whom we'll never meet.
- Technology allows us to meet with people without traveling.

Despite all this, SuperCompetent people seem to be able to magically recall conversations they had with people years ago. Their memories aren't better; they're simply more organized. They realize that to effectively organize their contacts with the people in their lives—both personal and professional—they must track contact information (phone, addresses, e-mail, and so on) and historical information (conversations, meetings, past/ upcoming communication, and so forth). They must be able to pull up the history on what was said to whom and when, without relying on memory.

Contact Information: What Is Your Name Again?

If you're in your car and need to call your dry cleaner, do you usually have the phone number on you? If you need to send out holiday cards and need to quickly print a set of labels for all your friends and relatives—but not clients—how long would it take you? To be organized, you must have systems for tracking the names, addresses, phone numbers, e-mail addresses, and other pertinent information about your clients, prospects, colleagues, contacts, friends, and family. This chapter will look at the different methodologies—paper-based, electronic, and hybrid—that can aid you in figuring out the best way to track your contacts' pertinent data.

1. *Paper Methods*. Paper planners, Rolodexes, and address books use paper methodologies to accomplish the same thing. Here are a few examples in common use.
   - *A–Z Tabs*. A–Z tabs in a traditional paper planner are great for tracking addresses and contact information—*if* you carry it with you at all times and don't have a lot of acquaintances

to track. My organization has 4,000 contacts in the ACT database where we keep business prospects and clients. Since it's nearly impossible to track those in paper, I only use my A–Z tabs in my planner for friends, family, and personal data I want to have on hand—such as bank, credit card, airline, and vendor information.

- One point to take into consideration: a paper reference method may be more useful than an electronic one when you are actually using your phone. While your contacts may be there at the touch of a button, how can you access them when you're already talking to someone? It's not impossible, but it can be a real pain.

- *Rolodex.* I still see some people using this traditional method of organizing information. The downside is the need to type out e-mail addresses when sending an e-mail, and a lack of portability when you travel. It works best for desk-bound individuals who rarely travel. But if you're a visual person and like to see the actual card you were handed, this might appeal to you.

- *Address book.* Many people who don't work outside the home (but who often work harder when they stay home!) still use a traditional paper address book. The most inflexible type is a spiral-bound version, in which the rings can't be opened and the pages moved around. When people move or drop out, there tend to be a lot of messy cross-outs and changes.

2. *Electronic Methods.* Contact management software such as Outlook, ACT, and Goldmine allow you to quickly store, search, and report on various contacts or groups of records. Syncing to your handheld device allows for immediate recall of this information—anywhere, anytime. Mail merge allows you to send out mailings and create labels with Word and Excel.

3. *Hybrid Methods.* If you don't have a handheld, you could keep all your contact information in Outlook or other contact management software at work and then print out address book pages to take home. Investigate the options under File/Print/Address book. Then you'd have all the data in one place and still accessible when you're out of the office. It's important to avoid a situation where you find yourself saying, "I need to call Jane, but her contact information is at work."

History: Where Were You, and What Did You Say?

When a contact calls, can you instantly pull up all related information to that person: e-mails, tasks, meeting requests, appointments, phone calls, and conversations? If you hear from a colleague, do you instantly know the five things you needed to discuss? When it's time for your weekly one-on-one meeting with your assistant, can you instantly pull up a list—with corresponding documentation—of all items to review with him? If you go to a restaurant with a client and don't have anything to write on, what do you grab? A napkin? The back of an old grocery list? If you don't have this information readily available at your fingertips, you'll be searching your sent e-mail records or spending 30 minutes hunting for a little piece of paper with notes from a luncheon meeting. The following tactics are a little less embarrassing and hugely more effective.

1. *Paper Methods.* No matter how nifty or high-tech, handhelds are generally useless for taking notes. It's hard to type quickly on those tiny keyboards, which is why most people still turn to paper. If you don't have a consistent place to write notes, you'll pick up the most convenient paper around and end up being a "scrapper" with odd pieces of paper everywhere. If this is how you take notes, fine, but make sure that you take the time to enter the information into the history section of the contact's record in your management system when you have a chance. Then you can toss the note.
   - *Lined Pages.* My Productivity Pro® planner by Day-Timer comes with a flexible note-taking method. You can grab a new blank Note page and take notes during a meeting with a client, and then file the note behind the A–Z tab for the client, or keep it in your daily pages for future reference. I also use my A–Z tabs in my paper planner as a filing system to track communications with people and things I need to remember to tell them. Use plain, lined paper the same size as your planner. Write the name of each person with whom you communicate frequently at the top; as you think of things you need to discuss with others, simply turn to the person's log and make a note of it.

- *Spiral notebook*. Notebooks with a spiral binding tend to get all sorts of various notes mixed up. It's better to use a spiral notebook with movable pages, such as the Circa system (available at www.levenger.com).
- *Three-ring binder or project folder*. For each new project or committee you're on, use a binder with tabbed sections or a hanging folder to store your notes. All you need to add pages is a three-hole punch.

2. *Electronic Methods*. Office productivity software offers a wide variety of ways to keep track of conversations and your history with your contacts. Some are specifically designed for this. For example, my company uses ACT software to track all conversations and e-mails we have with clients. After talking with someone on the phone, we type up all our manual notes into the person's record. This way, anyone on our staff can see what anyone else recently discussed with the client.

- Outlook offers two tools for doing the same thing, one being the Journal—a little-used feature that helps you relate items to a Contact by creating links. It also keeps track of your activities during the day, or if you create a Task to call several of your clients, you can use the Contacts button to link the task to those contacts in the task item.
- Or you could use the Notes feature in Outlook to keep a running list of items to discuss with a particular person. You'd tag the Note with the Contact name. Then, when you connect with that person, you'd open their Contact record and click the Activities tab, and then the Notes tab, to pull up the list of items to discuss.

3. *Hybrid Methods*. Another option is to print out your Journal entries and Notes and file them behind the appropriate A–Z tab in a paper planner.

Where's That Card Again . . . ?

All business is based on relationships. Unless you live in a cave somewhere (and maybe even if you do), you're part of a web of contacts that help you find, expedite, and get work done. So keeping track of those contacts is a must. After all, if you're a rare book dealer and you can't remember the name of the guy who offered you the first edition Dickens novel back in July, you may as well not even have met him.

Unlike the bigwigs, many of us don't have living organizers—that is, assistants—to keep track of our contacts. Fortunately, all it takes is a little time here and there to put together and maintain a contacts list; whether it consists of the enormous Rolodexes my old manager used to use, or the nifty features Outlook and handhelds provide. They're there for a reason, so take the time to learn how to use them fully. You'll be glad you did.

CHAPTER 20

On the Road
Again . . .

SUPERCOMPETENT Hero Thinking:	I don't waste time while traveling; I'm efficient and get a lot accomplished.
SIMPLY COMPETENT Zero Thinking:	I'm just going to take a nap on the plane. I can get all that stuff done later.

I fly over 100,000 miles a year on United Airlines. It's a job hazard as a professional speaker. Parts of it I hate, and some things I enjoy, such as working uninterrupted on a plane. I know not everyone has the natural ability to live out of a suitcase or do business from a laptop bag. However, with a little practice, you can learn how to make the most of your travel time. It's amazing what you can get done when you put some miles between yourself and the usual distractions of everyday life.

This chapter will share tips to help you make the most of your time away. I hope a few of them will help you become as productive when you're away from the office as you are when you're there.

The Plane Is My Mobile Office

If you were fortunate enough to have ever met the late Art Berg, CSP, CPAE, you have truly been blessed. This pioneer of using technology in a way that helps people simplify their lives was the founder of the Internet calendaring system I use: www .espeakers.com. Art always told me, "Never waste your time on the plane. The more you get done while you're traveling, the more time you'll have available to be with your family when you return." I took his sage advice to heart and now *plan* on being able to knock out a bunch of work while I'm away from home. I don't sleep, rent movies, or listen to music on the plane—I *work*. I read business journals, trade magazines, write thank-you letters, complete routine paperwork, create Power-Point presentations, review large reports and board materials, or do project and advance planning.

Take your office into the air and hotel, and tell yourself, "This is my uninterrupted time. There's no one else to take care of but myself. I'm going to use it to get ahead."

Pack Efficiently

It all starts with being organized and thinking ahead. Did you ever stay up half the night packing, and then spend an entire trip frustrated, exhausted, and wondering what it was you forgot? Don't let that happen again. Though trips rarely pop up at the last minute, they do have a way of sneaking up on you. Instead of packing the day before (especially for longer conferences), start thinking about your trip several days in advance.

Find an out-of-the-way spot to leave an open suitcase and drop things in as you think of them. When it's time to get ready to go, you'll be practically done. Keep a toiletries or one-quart Ziploc bag with duplicate items of *everything*, so you only have to pack outfits. One of my speaker colleagues, Rebecca Morgan, photographs her entire outfit at home—shoes, jewelry, purse, and so on—so she can quickly pull together what she needs at the hotel. I have a rotating set of 8–10 outfits—including jewelry and accessories—that I wear for traveling and speeches. I only wear St. John knits on the platform, because they pack easily, don't wrinkle, require no ironing, are as comfortable as pajamas, and look great. When I'm flying, I wear the Travelers line by Chicos. Again, no ironing, no wrinkling, and machine wash/dry. Guys, keep your ties, belts, shoes, and so forth, together in your closet, and wrap your dry-cleaned shirts in the plastic bags they come in, which will help with wrinkling. I keep all outfits in one location together, so I don't have to search. As long as you don't see the same people over and over again, you don't have to wear something different each trip. Find favorite outfits and make it easy on yourself.

Don't Check Your Briefcase or Laptop

Obviously, it's best to pack a carry-on if at all possible. I can use a carry-on for a trip of several days but usually have to surrender and check bags for a week-long conference. But *always* carry your essential business information. Stuff happens. Bags disappear—usually not permanently, but for long enough to make you wish you had them. While there's not a whole lot you can do if this happens, you can at least be confident your computer and other work essentials are close at hand. Don't be tempted to tuck a stack of folders in with your suitcase. If there's a baggage mishap, you can probably handle business in yesterday's clothes, but not without your files. When I'm forced to check a bag, I wear business casual instead of jeans or casual clothes. In the rare instance I end up without baggage, I can give my presentation in my travel clothes. Audiences are generally understanding and normally don't notice. Hey, it's happened to all of us.

Have a Plan Before Your Trip

You'll usually have a pretty good idea of how much downtime you'll have during your trip, so set some goals for your travel time before you leave. How long is the flight each way? How long will you be alone in your hotel room in the evening? Know what you want to accomplish during various parts of your trip. It isn't set in stone—it's just a guide. When you sit down in your airplane seat, you should know exactly what to do next. Maybe there's a report you want to read or a proposal you want to write. Be ready to dive right in. Until I can turn on my computer, I generally do light reading as I catch my breath and get settled. I might even do a Sudoku puzzle. Then I get right to it. I *never* turn on the television in my hotel, since a quiet hotel room is a great place to bang out work.

Embrace the Smart Phone (in Moderation)

You don't need to become a full-fledged CrackBerry addict to enjoy the benefits of a smart phone. It shouldn't hijack your life, but it *can* be a useful tool while you're riding in a taxi or sitting at the gate. Use your downtime to keep up with e-mail; it's comforting to know it isn't piling up while you're away. A smart phone can also help you stay on top of things back at the office without playing phone tag and leaving voicemails all over the place.

Use a Jump/Thumb Drive, Just in Case

It's tiny, inexpensive, and in a pinch, it just might save your career. These little gadgets can go right on your keychain, or for the truly paranoid, around your neck for safekeeping. You can use it as an emergency backup for files essential to your trip. If your laptop is stolen, your battery is fried, or you come face-to-face with the infamous Blue Screen of Death, you'll have a backup of your files—like the presentation you came so far to deliver. I had a computer refuse to start up once but was immediately able to upload my PowerPoint presentation to the client's laptop and carry on.

Simplify with a Docking Station

Do you find yourself transferring files between a desktop computer and your laptop when you need to travel or bring work home? This was one of my biggest frustrations and time wasters for many years. Unless your work requires some serious computer resources, you can probably stop using the desktop machine altogether. A docking station will allow you to keep your nice big monitor and full-size keyboard, but you'll still be able to pop your computer out of the dock, slip it into your laptop bag, and have all your files in one place. It's the best of both worlds.

Access Your Computer Remotely

If taking your computer with you isn't an option, consider setting up remote access. Some companies provide this through a virtual

network, or similar technology is available through sites like www
.gotomypc.com or www.logmein.com. As long as you have Internet access, you'll be able to get to the files and programs on your
computer. Once you're connected, you can operate your PC just
as if it were right in front of you.

Load Up a Phone Card

Hotel telephone fees can be outrageous, and cell-phone service
can leave you hanging when you least expect it. I've often been
without reception from my hotel room, couldn't get an Internet
connection (to use Skype), and had to use the landline. Get a pre-
paid phone card or calling-card service so you can make calls from
your room without racking up phone charges—or wandering
around the parking lot searching for a signal.

Pick Up an Extra Set of Chargers and Connectors

Keep them in your laptop bag or briefcase. This way, all of the
cords for all your gadgets—cell phone, PDA, Bluetooth, and laptop computer—are always packed and ready to go. When you arrive back to your office, you don't have to unpack all your cords.
My sets are permanently plugged in my office *and* stored in my
briefcase.

Use the Latest Tools and Technology

Of course, you have to stay in touch with your home and office to
be productive. Without a good cell phone plan, for example, you'll
hesitate to make long-distance calls. If you keep your Outlook calendar at work but don't have a printed copy or a PDA with you, it's
more difficult to plan. If you don't have wireless Internet and a
hot-spot subscription, you can't easily connect. It's worth paying
whatever the hotel charges to get wireless access in your room.
If you keep up with phone calls, e-mail, and clients while traveling, you won't have a pile of correspondence waiting for you
when you return.

Get EVDO

If you *must* have Internet access wherever you are, EVDO—
Evolution Data Optimized—with an aircard provides high-speed
Internet access through certain wireless networks such as Sprint or
Verizon. It's like using WiFi without searching for a hot spot. If
you pay for connection charges a few times a month in a hotel, the
convenience is worth the price tag. Get the necessary tools and
equipment to keep up with the office. You'll never need to make
the excuse, "I was on the road."

Get Personal Broadband

Portable WiFi, like Verizon's MiFi, is a recent breakthrough in
telephony, which lets you piggyback on high-broadband wireless
networks to access the Internet. Basically, you carry a tiny little
box about the size of a cell phone in your pocket, and you can
access the Internet anywhere there's a cell tower. It costs $40 to
$60 a month after paying $100 for the receiver. Beware, though,
of strangers wanting to access your portable network—and they
will try. It's not worth it to risk your security.

Carry a Pocket Folder or Portfolio

We're not talking about running around the office where you can
juggle fistfuls of papers until you get back to your desk. Conference papers, meeting notes, proposals, and sales receipts can all
end up crushed, mangled, or lost if you don't have someplace to
put them. Keep everything together and organized until you get
back from your trip. I create an envelope for each client meeting
and carry a seven-pocket Pendaflex folder for conferences, with
the documents I need separated by day.

Finish One Trip Before Starting the Next

Try not to load up your schedule the morning you return to the
office. You need time to unpack, reorganize, and process all information through your system and get it into the right place upon

your return. Unpack as soon as you get back. Fill lotions and toiletries so you have them ready for the next trip. Immediately reorganize your briefcase and office. Write reports and complete documentation while the information is fresh in your mind. Prepare expense reports or invoices for reimbursement immediately, so you get every dime you're entitled to receive. Otherwise, you'll soon get confused about what goes with what when you stack multiple trips back-to-back. If you don't schedule too much very close to your return, you'll feel more confident during your travels, because you've got some breathing space when you return.

Spending Money Means Saving Time

I don't drive to/from the airport. Some may think it's a bit lavish, but I create more value in working for two hours than I pay the driver. Plus, I avoid the stress of finding a parking spot, walking to the terminal, and paying for parking toll charges. Stick with one preferred airline to gain the highest status possible. Airline club access is important for the best travel experience (I pay for United's Red Carpet Club). Upgrade to rental car gold aisle (or equivalent) to avoid waiting in lines.

Preparation Is the Key to . . . Preparedness

Always bring a clean copy of any important documents or a thumb drive in case your laptop crashes. Bring an empty water bottle to fill when you get past security. Use a GPS to avoid stress in unfamiliar places (I use the Garmin Nuvi).

A Second Saved Is a Second Earned

There are so many small ways to make life easier for yourself when you're traveling, not just by laying the groundwork before you leave, but also by spending your travel time more effectively. I hope the tips outlined in this chapter will help you spend your time on the road more productively, and more importantly, leave you with less to do when you return home—so you can squander more time reuniting with your loved ones.

SUMMARY: ACCESSIBILITY

How much time do you spend every day trying to track things down—whether it's the location of the meeting starting in five minutes, the tasks you need to do today, or the phone number for a certain productivity expert you want to invite to your next meeting? While searching for these details might not take much time, it does force you to relinquish your focus. And once gone, it takes awhile to get it back, which is where the *real* time is wasted.

When perfectly fine-tuned to your needs, your time management system allows you to access the information you need exactly when you need it. Your calendar, lists, contact information are all immediately accessible, wherever you are. Your e-mail inbox is under control and emptied at least daily.

Another potential Accessibility related time-stealer is travel, but it doesn't have to be. When you have to spring into action at a moment's notice, it's easy to forget something important you need, which puts you in the red from the beginning, in terms of time. But if you practice some forethought and have your basics ready to go at anytime, it's up, up, and away, without having to worry if you've packed enough socks.

It's tempting to just lie back and relax while you're in transit, especially since travel can be so hectic and tense. But just a few minutes here and there can allow you to get a little something done, even if you don't have the time to focus like you might in your office. If nothing else, you can get the tasks, like managing and updating your contacts, out of the way, so you can spend more time enjoying your life when you're back home. And you might find working diligently makes your traveling less tiring—and certainly less boring.

Go to www.TheProductivityPro.com/Accessibility to receive bonus material, the SuperCompetent Key 4 assessment questions, a summary, and the action-planning worksheet in Microsoft Word format. Get additional resources, audios, videos, and more at www.SuperCompetentBook.com.

ACTION PLANNING WORKSHEET: ACCESSIBILITY

16. I've created the perfect time-management system for my personality, job environment, and work situation.
   What came to mind when I read this?

   _____
   _____
   _____
   _____

   What is my action plan for improvement?

   _____
   _____
   _____
   _____

17. I know exactly where I'm supposed to be and exactly what I should be working on at all times.
   What came to mind when I read this?

   _____
   _____
   _____
   _____

   What is my action plan for improvement?

   _____
   _____
   _____
   _____

18. My e-mail is organized, and my inbox is regularly emptied.
   What came to mind when I read this?

   _____
   _____
   _____
   _____

What is my action plan for improvement?

_____
_____
_____
_____

19. I keep careful track of my contacts and my communications with them; I can tell you what was said in a meeting a year ago.

What came to mind when I read this?

_____
_____
_____
_____

What is my action plan for improvement?

_____
_____
_____
_____

20. I don't waste time while traveling; I'm efficient and get a lot accomplished.

What came to mind when I read this?

_____
_____
_____
_____

What is my action plan for improvement?

_____
_____
_____
_____

PART 5

SuperCompetent Key 5: Accountability

SuperCompetent people take personal responsibility for their actions and outcomes.

ACCOUNTABILITY recognizes "the buck stops here."

This key teaches you to question processes, strive for continuous improvement, and practice self-discipline.

SuperCompetent people mean what they say and say what they mean. They make and follow through on promises to others. Other people know and appreciate their authenticity, as well as their refusal to blame others when unforeseen circumstances trip them up. SuperCompetent people are driven by an intense focus on their values, which are borne out of their demeanor and sense of accountability. A SuperCompetent person definitely honors Harry S. Truman's favorite expression: "The buck stops here."

Accountability involves a personal commitment to yourself and others; it's about the promises you make to the people who rely on you. Although developing your personal boundaries depends on your internal commitments, accountability is also about following through on your *external* commitments to others. This is the most difficult part of personal responsibility. However, when you're able to consistently hit goals, meet deadlines, and fulfill the promises you make to others, colleagues will perceive you as a responsible person. Becoming SuperCompetent requires mastery for its own sake, but having an excellent reputation is also helpful.

Dave Kutayia, Senior Vice President of Human Resources in ING Clarion's real estate investment division says, "Great employees are natural team players due to their strong value system and high work ethic. They're internally driven, with high standards and principles, so they get annoyed when people aren't carrying their weight." The lesson here: Personal responsibility is easy to observe in people who have it.

CHAPTER 21

Accept the Credit When It's Due— and the Blame, Too

SUPERCOMPETENT Hero Thinking:	I take personal responsibility for handling my time and productivity; I never lay the blame on anyone else.
SIMPLY COMPETENT Zero Thinking:	It's not my fault—I'm being pulled in too many directions at once!

I've been speaking about personal productivity for 18 years, long before it was even a topic. Before I get in front of any audience to give a presentation, I ask my client to send out a simple ten-point e-mail survey to a random sample of participants. The responses help me tailor my comments to the group and make sure I'm addressing the correct issues. One of the questions is, "What is the number one thing you would have to change about yourself if you were to be more productive?" And what kills me is that *everyone knows the answer*. So do you. But you don't do it, and neither do they. *Why?*

I've heard every excuse in the book. I watch people point fingers. I marvel at corporate policies that sabotage their employees. And just when I think to myself, "Now I *have* seen it all," I'll see something even more unbelievable a few weeks later. I've tried to be politically correct and smile and say something polite to poor or nonperformers, when all I want to say to some people is: "GET OFF YOUR BUTT AND WORK!"

There. I said it. This is why I turn down most personal coaching requests: Most people can't handle the truth. "Get off your butt" is certainly not a nice thing to say, so it doesn't fit me. But I tire of trying to nicely say what some people desperately need to hear. And secretly, many people have *wished* I'd said it to a coworker, subordinate, spouse, or friend. It's taken me years to say it, because it's going to take a gutsy leader to hire me to speak on the topic of Get Off Your Butt. Who wants to tell their people, "Hey, you're all a bunch of slackers, so we're bringing in the productivity consultant to whip all of you into shape and tell you why you stink as employees"? That message probably wouldn't resonate.

But those of you who *truly* understand the underlying premise get my purpose: To help people become the best they can be—and then get out of their own way. I'm looking for those with absolutely no patience for excuses, mediocrity, and finger pointing.

Jeff Arnold, Master Association Management (MAM), Executive Director of the Sales Association, says: "Although no one is indispensible, the ones who are closest to it are those who provide 'employer utility.' Although I had an ownership mindset rather than an employee mindset when I was an employee, I didn't get a real appreciation for those who had an owner mindset until I became a business owner myself. Many people who get jobs don't understand how every action they take affects the profitability of the company. They see their employer as little more than an ATM machine and their job as just a job. Employees who treat your business as if it were their own are the ones you want to hang on to. They add value, rather than just doing the tasks outlined in their job description. Even if they perform the job description exceedingly well, in times when you need innovation, 'employee mind-set' workers will only provide more of the same, nothing new that adds value. I see these types of workers as entirely dispensable, a dime a dozen. In tough times, they'll be the first to go."

Here are some actual excuses I've heard people utter—which you must stop using at once if you have used them:

- *I don't have the right training.* Get the training you need! Take the day off. Go to a class and pay for it yourself.
- *I don't have the right tools.* Buy the BlackBerry yourself! Bring your own printer from home and plug it in.
- *The lighting is bad.* Buy a lamp.
- *I'm too cold.* Bring a space heater.
- *I'm hot.* Bring a fan.

In other words: Take responsibility for yourself. How?

Master the Necessary Knowledge

Fill in the blanks on your own weaknesses and knowledge. Mastering your core task is pivotal in performing consistently and specifically requires the continual and consistent refinement of your fundamental competencies and skills. Investing in your knowledge may involve reading, listening to audio programs, attending conferences, or participating in professional organizations and workshops. Whatever the case, you need to develop a consistent hunger for brain food that will impress your superiors and coworkers. Hone the skills needed to perform your job, and work *above* what's required on a daily basis—don't just skate by because you *can*.

Fine-Tune Your Behavior

If I ask about someone's competence, I'm also asking about his or her consistency. No SuperCompetent person is competent only *some* of the time; SuperCompetents are trustworthy, timely, and reliable *all* the time. Everyone assumes they'll come through every time, not just occasionally or when it suits them. People make these assumptions based on past experience. To be SuperCompetent, you must learn how to deliver and *never* disappoint.

Get Feedback

Ask friends, coworkers, or even your boss what they feel are your strengths and weaknesses. Take this information and try to pinpoint the times where you fall short of what others expect of you. Do you spend too much time working on a single project? Are you 15 minutes late for work every day? You have the power to control both your assets and vulnerabilities. Learn from your mistakes and use your weakness to gain more strength by correcting problems in your performance as you see them arise.

Hone Your Ethics

SuperCompetent people are reliably honest, principled, and driven by doing the right thing. Sometimes mastering the art of ethics isn't as simple as it seems; gray areas can arise that send one's moral compass spinning with no clear direction. In later chapters of this book, I'll offer simple tools that can help you navigate your way through the ethical labyrinth.

Conquer OCSMD

I discussed this at length in Chapter 14, so I'll just issue a short warning here: Don't fall victim to Obsessive-Compulsive Social Media Disorder by checking your Facebook and Twittering all day. All electronic and social media doesn't need to be checked *right this minute* when you should be working. Motion is distracting, so turn off alerts, turn on rules, and stop worrying about what you'll miss. The same thing goes for all of your technology.

So . . . Are You Off Your Butt Yet?

As I mentioned at the beginning of this chapter, we all know one of the real reasons we're unproductive: We won't just buckle down and get to work. You'd be amazed at all the excuses I hear for not working. Well, you're not in your offices just to hold down the chair, so if something's getting in the way of your productivity, then fix it. Don't just complain and lay the blame on someone else; SuperCompetent people don't do this. Except for a few minor and rare circumstances, there's no one you can blame for your lack of productivity but *yourself.*

CHAPTER 22

The Squeaky Wheel . . . Makes Things Better

SUPERCOMPETENT Hero Thinking:	When I see an unusually lengthy and inefficient process, I do what I can to make it easier for everyone.
SIMPLY COMPETENT Zero Thinking:	There's no need to change our way of doing things. If it was good enough for Grandpa, it's good enough for me.

You sometimes have to stop and take a closer look at the systems and processes you're using in the business world to determine whether they're still working as they were originally intended. Too often, people just accept how they've been taught to do something rather than considering whether it could be improved. But situations and technology change, and sometimes we fail to change with them.

Dave Kutayia explains, "When deciding on whether to hire one person over another, I [assume that] both candidates possess the requisite Knowledge, Skills, and Abilities (KSAs) necessary to do the job. They represent [that] they have the skills and then they demonstrate it through their efforts. Which one is going to know his or her limitations and continually work to improve? They're not a proven entity to me and essentially sell me a promise. I want to hear about where they've given over-and-above effort in the past. They may be naturally gifted, but I want to know they're driven and want to do the job well."

Instead of saying, "It's the way we've always done it," or concluding "This won't work," SuperCompetent people ask, "What needs to happen to *make* this work?" They're full of possibility, always asking, "Why not?" instead of "Why?" This positivity makes their efforts more likely to succeed from the beginning. When motivating others, they're likely to use phrases such as: take a risk; begin with the end in mind; results rule; learn optimism; challenges are temporary; you can fix it; and take initiative. They do their homework, even in areas that don't come naturally, and when faced with limits to their own knowledge, they get the training needed to move forward. They learn to take opportunities for improvement, rather than shying away or denying the need.

Unfortunately, there are hordes of people who believe it's more important to blindly follow the rules, letter by letter, than to do what's best or most effective. As Ralph Waldo Emerson pointed out, "A foolish consistency is the hobgoblin of little minds."

Here's a more prosaic example of how the Simply Competent can muck things up for the rest of us by being foolishly consistent. I have a love/hate relationship with United Airlines. I fly frequently, so I have special status and earn lots of miles. These miles have given my family and me several wonderful vacations over the years, so I'm not complaining too loudly. *But.* I had planned a family trip using miles to Hawaii in October. I bought my ticket, so I'd get the miles (you don't get miles on a free ticket), and used 40,000 miles each for my other four family members, subtracting 160,000 miles, and effectively wiping out my account.

Imagine my delight when I got an e-mail from United, announcing the Mileage Plus Saver Award mileage sale! If you flew between August 18 and November 18, you could get tickets to Hawaii for only 30,000 per ticket! Woo-hoo—we were going in October—I qualified! Ten thousand miles saved on each ticket would mean I could get 40,000 miles credited back to my account. Sweet! So I called my special secret 1K mileage-plus phone number. I got an agent and explained, "Hi, I just received an e-mail about your mileage sale. I have a trip booked in that time frame and would like to be credited for the difference in the miles."

To my surprise, he told me, "The sale is only good on trips not already booked." So I said, "Wait a minute. You're going to reward the procrastinators for not booking their trips, and people who plan ahead are penalized?" He said, "Ma'am, you're not being penalized, you just can't have a credit." I said, "Wait. When I purchase a ticket, and discover later the fare went down, I can call you and get a credit for the difference, which is what I'm doing now." He said, "Ma'am, it doesn't work that way for this promotion; it's only new trips. As a 1K member, there are no penalties for me to redeposit the miles, and you can just rebook it discount fare."

I said, "You mean to tell me United would waste your time canceling a flight, depositing the miles, rebooking the flight, and taking out the miles again? What a convoluted process! I just want you to credit 40,000 miles to my account! I am one of your best flyers! You call this customer service? This is a huge waste of my time!" He said, "Yes, ma'am, correct, and by the way, if I put the miles back, in that time someone would probably grab your seats, and then there would no longer be any mileage seats available." You've got to be kidding me! At which point, I asked for a supervisor, explained the issue, and was told exactly the same thing. He then said, "I highly recommend you write to United Airlines and complain." What?! You work there! It's this type of absolute craziness that makes no sense in organizations. All this did was inconvenience one of their best customers, waste staff time, and practice crazy making!

You can't follow the letter of the law in all circumstances. People have to be empowered to make decisions when the process makes no sense. Here are some suggestions on how you can accomplish it—whether you're the boss or not.

Create a Process to Simplify the Task

Quite often, the time traps that drive us crazy stem from something being done inefficiently. If you're struggling with the same or similar tasks over and over, it's time to get a system in place; think *process*. Could you make a template for the letter or report you're now rewriting for the umpteenth time? Are you overwhelmed by your weekly filing? Perhaps you might consider handling paperwork as it comes in, before it piles up? Could you figure out how to print directly on the envelope or use labels if you're constantly handwriting addresses?

The same is true at home. Could your family be more diligent about getting their dirty clothes to the laundry area in an orderly fashion? Dinner, laundry, paying bills, endless chores. Developing a system can dramatically reduce the frustration caused by everyday tasks. A reusable checklist could keep you moving in the right direction. No thinking, no reprioritizing; just start at the top of your list and cross things off until you get to the bottom. Just as runners finish marathons one stride at a time, you'll get through your list with diligent perseverance. Just take it one item at a time, until you're all the way through.

Complete the Task in Less Time

Sometimes we're so busy looking for an extra 30 minutes to complete a task we don't realize it could be done in 10. Make sure you aren't overresearching, overanalyzing, or just plain overthinking what you're trying to do.

Some fish will grow to fit the size of their tank, and tasks will do the same thing. If you're convinced putting the groceries away always takes 45 minutes, then it always will. If Step 1 of writing a report is always an hour of banging your head against the blank computer screen, it becomes the norm.

Don't fall into this trap. Evaluate your tasks and challenge yourself to get them done more quickly. If you had to have the report written by the end of the day instead of the end of the week, you would find a way to get it done. Tight deadlines don't leave much time for banging your head on the computer. When a crisis pops up, rise to the challenge. Apply the same never-say-die attitude to your more routine tasks, and you'll be amazed at what you can accomplish.

Focus, Focus, Focus

What's the number-one technique for speeding things up? *Focus*. Give yourself 10 minutes to concentrate on the task at hand. Once you commit your full energy to getting it done, you'll be amazed at how things start zipping along. By eliminating distractions and taking a break from multitasking, you'll put an end to those unproductive minutes—which can fly by when you're trying to do too many things at once.

Don't Forget About Technology

We take technology for granted in our day-to-day lives, but for all the hassles it can bring us, it provides some real time-savers as well. Don't be afraid to invest a few minutes in learning to use Outlook templates for common responses or e-mails. Or if your Internet connection is dragging you down, consider upgrading to a speedier connection. Have you been meaning to start paying bills online? Make yourself a cup of tea and get those accounts set up once and for all. There's lots of time to be saved by investing in faster ways of doing things.

Try to Change the Scope

Projects snowball and to-do items multiply. You have no idea how it happened, but you're sure the task at hand has gotten much more complicated than when you first started. Maybe a casual office brainstorm turned into a corporate strategy think tank. Or perhaps tidying up the flowerbed became a major landscaping project. Take a deep breath and get back on track by refocusing on your original intentions. Once your work is done, you can take another look at the big picture.

Streamline Your Life

In almost every case, there was once a logical reason for why you do things the way you do, either at home or work. Sometimes, though, that logical reason no longer applies; you occasionally need to take a step back. Examine the individual processes and subprocesses and determine whether you've been handling them in the most effective way. You may discover there's no longer a reason to perform a particular task in the first place, so don't hesitate to get rid of it. See how you can accomplish just as much by doing less, so you can leave the office earlier and enjoy your life.

CHAPTER 23

Crack That Whip!

SUPERCOMPETENT Hero Thinking:	Rather than waste even small amounts of time, I get right to work.
SIMPLY COMPETENT Zero Thinking:	Whew! That was exhausting. I need a break! I'll go get a cup of coffee and say hello to my friend Susan.

Self-discipline is important in any field of endeavor. Do you complete a task within a certain time frame when you promise someone you will? Or does the deadline slip past with you muttering to yourself, "Stupid! What is *wrong* with you?" Now you aren't able to focus on anything, always aware of this dark cloud hanging over your head. Guilt sucks the energy right out of you!

Instead, decide today to be a person of your word. How do other people perceive you? Are you reliable? Can people count on you to do what you say you're going to do? Do you have integrity and keep the deadlines you promise? Do you live out what you affirm? Do you do what you complain about in others? What things do people jokingly say about you and your behavior?

Learn to control yourself and your habits. If you say to yourself, "I probably shouldn't be doing this right now," you're probably right. Be honest with yourself: How many hours could you save every day by being more disciplined? Could you leave the office earlier with that saved time? If tomorrow you arrived at work and didn't get a cup of coffee, didn't get on the Internet, didn't talk to your friend, didn't get sucked into e-mail for 90 minutes . . . where could you use the extra energy that would make you proud and give you a boost of satisfaction for the entire day?

When you finally complete the task you've been putting off, the freedom from the stress it was causing is its own reward. Good things begin to flow into the space the guilt used to occupy. You're no longer paralyzed, and you get your energy back.

So cut out the time you waste each day on nonproductive activities. Eliminate anything that doesn't have long-term consequences for your work. Philosopher William James once wrote, "The art of being wise is the art of knowing what to overlook." In addition to a to-do list each day, have a *not*-to-do list containing your personal discipline rules. Always do what needs to be done, even if you don't feel like it.

Procrastination: Can We Talk About This Later?

Sometimes we don't get things done because we can't seem to get the ball rolling. While a challenging project might be within our control, we simply don't make it happen. Whether the task is intimidating, time-consuming, or simply unpleasant, the solution is often the same: Break it down into manageable chunks to make it easier to get started.

Forget waiting for a block of time—it no longer exists. Schedule the individual stages of the project across a period of a week or two. A 20-hour project can be seen as ten 2-hour tasks, for example. Getting it down on paper can help you see how to best approach it. The key is just to *do something* to move toward completion. Rather than feeling like you have to tackle some monumental project all at once, you can just look at your bite-sized first step and get started right away.

The Early Bird Gets the Worm; the Tardy Bird Gets . . . Eaten Alive

One of the most common complaints I hear from leaders who bring me in to speak to their employees on performance involves "the inability to meet deadlines, always being late, constantly running behind, or being forgetful."

People are much more irritated by lateness than you can know or they will admit; it can dampen everything from promotions and raises to friendships. Late people crowd you, physically and mentally. When people fail to show up on time, it undoes your schedule and disrupts your day. Showing up late or sending something in late—no matter how well done—still means a black mark against you.

I'm blessed to be close friends with leadership speaker and author Mark Sanborn and his wife, Darla. Since we live only a few miles apart and both have young boys, our families frequently enjoy spending time together. At a recent Fourth of July barbeque at our home, Mark teased me (a not-uncommon occurrence) about the already-cut-up plates of tomatoes, onions, pickles, and lettuce, wrapped in plastic, waiting in the refrigerator for the burgers. I joked back, "Why, I'm just following the Principle of Preparation from your book *The Encore Effect*!" Does the simple act of slicing burger fixings in advance make for a better barbeque? I think so. Being unprepared would have meant trying to cut everything up while the burgers got cold. I still would have been on time, but I'd be half listening to them and missing pieces of conversation while focusing on my task. It simply didn't occur to me to *not* cut everything in advance.

This is the source of many people's lateness: They're trying to do things and be on time. Sanborn defines average performance as, "the best of the worst and the worst of the best." He explains further, "These performers are the best of the mediocre middle, neither hot nor cold but lukewarm. The problem is average performance doesn't get you noticed." I couldn't agree more! Simply being on time is fairly typical. It just doesn't stand out. It's okay . . . it's just expected . . . yawn.

Don't be simply average! Don't be on time. Be EARLY. Be in advance, proactive, and looking forward. Take a long-term focus. We're not talking ridiculously early here; don't inconvenience your host by showing up for a party three hours early. It's a way of thinking, a way of being, and a way to frame your behavior.

Find a Reasonable Work-Life Balance

Life happens, and it isn't always convenient; some things can only be arranged during the week from 9:00 to 5:00. Fortunately, companies are starting to realize it's in their best interest to assist— rather than hinder—employees' attempts to manage their lives. This can mean anything from allowing workers to access the Internet for incidental personal use to offering flexible schedules to accommodate personal appointments.

Talk to your boss, your peers, and your staff about finding opportunities for flexibility within the workday. If employees don't feel like they have to accomplish a million things during five lunch hours a week, they'll be more productive during the rest of the day. Do whatever you can to promote a strong, reasonable work-life balance at your organization.

Working on Mundane Tasks and Not-Fun Things

I've already discussed how we often put off large or overwhelming projects, but what about the small, mundane tasks you just can't seem to get motivated to complete? The best thing you can do is realize you'll focus much better on your important work if you don't have a bunch of small, less interesting duties hanging over your head. About 99 percent of the time, those chores are dramatically easier and less painful than you think they're going to be. Getting started is the hardest part. If you're having trouble, schedule a five-minute appointment with yourself to begin the chore. When the designated time arrives, start working on the task. If you feel like stopping at the end of five minutes, you can stop. The only rule is you must schedule an additional five minutes for tomorrow. When you begin to see some progress, five minutes soon becomes 10, 15, 20, . . . and soon enough, it's done!

Put Perfection in Its Place

You might pride yourself on your perfectionism, but everything has a time and a place. A year-end report? Fine—cross every *t* and dot every *i*. The routine status report no one reads? Relax. Your time is too valuable to stress over the small stuff. Sometimes, your task needs to be as close to perfect as humanly possible. Other times, you just need to get the job done. Some tasks demand excellence, while some only need to be acceptable. Know when to give your inner perfectionist a well-deserved rest.

Besides, perfectionism is a dangerous path; be careful! Perfection is never going to happen. While some people take great pride in their perfectionist personas, they carry around a lot of baggage as a result. So many things will just never be good enough, which leads to some counterproductive trends and a lot of negative energy. A perfectionist's projects are often in a frustrating limbo. The quality of the work is through the roof, but the project will sit untouched and incomplete for weeks. If this sounds like you, then the sooner you break the cycle, the better.

Give Yourself a Deadline

If your project lacks a deadline, create your own. For example, you will finish compiling your research by the end of this week; your first draft will be due the end of next week; and the third week will be free for some constructive collaboration, giving you time to tweak your final product. Just make sure to treat your timetable with the same respect and commitment you would devote to the unwavering deadline handed down by your boss.

Just Do It!

I was privileged to hear one of my speaking colleagues, Janet Lapp, PhD, CPAE, speak before a local Colorado chapter of the National Speakers Association. She talked to the group about their goals. "I talk to a speaker one year, who will say, 'I'm working on my book.' The next year? 'I'm working on my book.' They don't truly commit and don't see any forward progress. You want to write a book? Well, JUST DO IT and stop talking about it! You want to lose weight? JUST DO IT! Everyone knows what it takes: exercise more and eat less. It has nothing to do with your dysfunctional family or issues with your mother. Get over it and JUST DO IT."

I laughed aloud and applauded loudly, enthusiastically nodding my head in agreement.

Janet's point: When it comes to self-discipline, *you* are the boss. No one can get you to buckle down and get to work. Sure, they can order you to work, threaten you, or otherwise attempt to motivate you. However, when it comes down to it, you're not going to get anything done until and unless you decide to get moving, and the easiest way to get moving is to *never stop*. You may have heard of the Law of Inertia, which states that an object in motion tends to stay in motion, while an object at rest tends to stay at rest. While we all need down time, your best bet during the productive period of your day is to just *avoid shutting down*. Keep going! Don't go talk with your buddies or take care of family business unless it's unavoidable. Don't allow yourself to miss deadlines or otherwise be tardy. Not only are you stealing time from yourself, you're stealing it from others. Then *keep* moving when you get home. Don't plop down on the sofa to "rest"; you may never get up. SuperCompetents seem like perpetual motion machines. They allow themselves periodic breaks but are pretty much *always* moving.

If you're overwhelmed by the size of a task, break it into manageable portions and get to work. If you feel no sense of urgency because there's no deadline, create one.

What it all comes down to is what Nike suggests repeatedly in its advertisements: Just Do It. Don't procrastinate. Just Do It.

CHAPTER 24

Let's Get On With It!

SUPERCOMPETENT Hero Thinking:	When I have all the information I need to proceed, I make decisions quickly.
SIMPLY COMPETENT Zero Thinking:	I don't want to make this decision right now. What if I make a mistake? What if something goes wrong?

The SuperCompetent are able to make critical decisions wherever necessary. A caveat, of course, is you're empowered to make those decisions. You may not be empowered to decide to sell your company, but if it's up to you to decide on a new telephone system or photocopier, don't drag your feet. Get all the information you need, review it carefully, talk it over with the people affected by the decision and trusted advisors, and make your decision. Get on with it!

As motivational speaker Jim Cathcart, CSP, CPAE, wrote to me, "In my experience, those who succeed despite circumstances are those who *decide* to do so. It's simple. Not as easy as it sounds, but profoundly simple. When you decide not to let the situation dictate your future, you become more creative, give more of yourself and seek opportunities. When you do not make this decision, your attention denigrates into worry, fear, cynicism and depression. Choose to succeed, and the processes will reveal themselves as you progress."

Jim just described a SuperCompetent person: Tough-minded and unafraid to make difficult decisions. They address problems directly and think challenges through more fully than others do. They anticipate difficulties before they arise and don't let themselves become paralyzed by them—or even by thinking about them. They're action oriented and make things happen. They correct mistakes quickly and forge ahead without pointing fingers.

Wes Crocheron is a consultant with a master's degree in Counseling Psychology, and he worked in the aerospace industry for 20 years. He said the industry's culture included a reluctance to take responsibility for decisions, so one young engineer's willingness to be decisive stood out in a positive way: "One of the biggest problems with technical contributors is they're reluctant to disagree or make independent decisions. In aerospace, mistakes aren't looked on favorably, so keeping your nose clean is an institutional personality. Every issue was studied to death, and no one was willing to go out on a limb."

"But this young engineer didn't follow those rules. If he didn't agree with the position or direction the team was taking, he was decisive in speaking up, disagreeing, and saying why. He had the technical knowledge, but he was also willing to take the risk and stick his neck out on unpopular decisions. If he made a mistake, he owned up to it and fixed it. The customer would accept the product despite the deficiency, with his promise it would be fixed and handled. They trusted him and knew he would do what he said he would. I enjoyed watching him go far in his career."

Successful Decision-Making Tools

There are a few things you need to have or do to successfully make decisions, but these tools are easy to acquire and even easier to wield:

1. *Desire*. To become more decisive, you must first have the desire to *be* more decisive. Although this doesn't come naturally to everyone, it can be learned. We all struggle from time to time

with small decisions. However, SuperCompetence demands an ability to commit even to big decisions, and desire is a big factor in being committed. Research has shown people who believe they have the power to make a choice will handle the task more effectively.

2. *Practice.* The old saying "practice makes perfect" is a cliché for a good reason. To become a committed decision maker, you must first *practice* making decisions. Start with small things and work your way up.

3. *Analyze/Visualize.* When facing a decision, it's helpful to imagine how you'd respond to each possible outcome. By envisioning these scenarios, you can eliminate less-attractive options. Let's take a simple example: what to have for lunch. Tacos might be nice, but one possible result of eating them is a case of heartburn. Salad might also be nice, and it won't give you any painful side effects. Thinking about the potential outcomes has now helped you narrow the choice.

4. *Deadlines.* In the absence of time pressure, some decisions just don't get made. So set time limits on decisions to move them forward. Only allow yourself a limited amount of time to choose a certain course of action. Then give yourself less and less time as you become a better decision maker. You'll be able to commit to bigger tasks if you give yourself just enough time to analyze the situation well, but not enough to procrastinate.

Business speaker David Goldsmith offered me some great advice about decision making: "No one succeeds at every challenge they undertake. Winners in business do a few activities that make them succeed at what appears to be 'every challenge.' These individuals are great strategists. They can, either intuitively or through work, create both the strategy and tactics well enough that when they attack a challenge they succeed. They take the time to think. These individuals fail a lot, yet they don't market the failure as a failure to themselves or to others. They get up quickly and move on. This group learns from their experiences for future experiences. You may call it a postgame review. They play over in their mind the experience, take the lessons, and adjust the future. In all, they have an internal winning formula they strive to achieve."

Slippery Activities

What happens when things go wrong, priorities change, or activities slip? This happens to the best of us, so don't fret too much about the possibility. What's important is how you react and recover in such a circumstance. Here are some suggestions:

- Renegotiate a due date. There may be a couple of days of flexibility.
- Recover lost time in later steps. Reexamine time allocations.
- Narrow the scope of the project and eliminate nonessential items.
- Deploy more resources (in terms of people or machines). Weigh the cost against the importance of the deadline.
- Accept substitutions. Use a comparable item, if you must.
- Seek alternative sources. Switch suppliers.
- Accept partial delivery. Have subordinates and other departments give you enough to get you past the critical point.
- Offer incentives. To get someone you are depending on to put forth additional effort, offer a reward for on-time completion.
- Demand compliance. As a last resort, you may have to insist upon deliverance according to the agreement—or else.
- Appeal to a higher authority for guidance. Check with the boss if you're stumped or a project is going to be in trouble.

Get a Move On!

One of the biggest reasons people drag their feet is because they're unwilling or unable to make decisions. Sometimes this is because they would have to run up against other people in order to do so. Well, so be it. In any organization that numbers more than one, you're eventually going to be at loggerheads with someone else, no matter what you do. When this comes to pass, try to defuse any foot-dragging behavior.

When you've got all the information and resources you need to dive into a project or make a decision, there's no time to hesitate. So make the decision and move on it. Sure, you might make a mistake; it might not work out. That's life. As they say, nothing ventured, nothing gained.

You can't let indecision paralyze you. If you have to make a decision, make it, and do your best to avoid any possible negative consequences. Cultivate the desire to be decisive and get started. Begin with small decisions and work your way up to the big ones. As Larry the Cable Guy likes to put it, "Get 'er done!"

CHAPTER 25

Tweaking Time Wasters

SUPERCOMPETENT Hero Thinking:	I understand the difference between being busy and being productive: results.
SIMPLY COMPETENT Zero Thinking:	I've been working hard all day! What do you mean I wasn't productive?

What are you *really* assessing when you look at productivity? Simply put, you're looking at *results*. This is easier to measure in manufacturing: You just count whatever comes off the line. Business productivity is a little more difficult. Let's say that one person in an office works an 8-hour day and another person works a 12-hour day. Can the person working the 8-hour day be more productive than the 12-hour-a-day person? Yes, of course. It doesn't matter how many hours you sit there; you could have been checking your eBay listings, playing Minesweeper, or talking to your mom. Just because you were there doesn't mean you were producing or doing anything of value.

The 80/20 Principle

When we look at output, we're looking at results, profitability, value, worth, weight, or impact. Our inputs are all the things we can do. I'll use an easy example to explain this.

About a century ago, Italian economist Vilfredo Pareto noticed that 20 percent of the people in his country owned 80 percent of the wealth. He called this the "principle of the trivial many and the vital few" and later reformulated it as the easier-to-swallow "80/20 principle." Although it's a bit simplified, in most business situations, about 20 percent of your activities produce about 80 percent of the results; therefore, those activities should require 80 percent of your efforts.

So let's say you have a daily to-do list with only 10 things on it. (Wouldn't that be nice?) According to the 80/20 principle, two items on the list would be the most critical. Now, let's be honest: When you get a small block of discretionary time and look at your list, what are you tempted to do first? You *want* to do the easiest task, of course. It just feels good to check it off. This is completely understandable, given our human condition. If you're an office worker, when is the last time you ever left at the end of the day and said, "I'm done! I've finished everything!"? Have you *ever* finished? I can't remember, but I'm fairly sure I haven't finished in years.

In the old days, people were done at the end of the day. The payloads were delivered, the sheep were fed, and the fields were planted. It's still like this to some extent with line jobs and mail delivery. But for knowledge workers, there's always an impending sense of doom. You're *never* done. When I married my husband, he was a letter carrier. He went to work, delivered his pile of mail, and headed home. Clearly, he couldn't take it home with him (they would hunt him down if he did). So every day, John would be stress free; work began when he went into the post office, and ended, period, when he left.

Then in the year 2000, John came to work for my company as the Director of Marketing (he's now the COO). Do you ever finish marketing? Of course not. He would be working and working, stressing himself out, thinking about it at 2:00 in the morning, until he finally got comfortable with the difference between his old job and the new. You *never* finish knowledge work. You have to get used to this stressor—it's just a fact of life.

So when you cross something off your list and get that little psychological ding, it feels good. We get a sense of accomplishment from completion, no matter how small. Old time-management techniques taught people that the more things they checked off the list, the more productive they were. Let's say you got nine things done on a list of ten—whoa, you were busy. But what's usually left? The hardest thing—the one you don't want to do. And how long have you been putting it off now? A week? A month? Two months? How do you feel about it? Stressed, right? You think, "What's wrong with me? Why can't I get anything done? I've been working so hard all day! It isn't fair."

To simplify, for nonfarm, business workers, personal productivity is valued as output per hour, per worker. Output—not input. In other words, let's say I did eight things on a list of ten—everything but my two highest value items. I would be at 20 percent of my potential contribution for the same amount of time, given what my responsibilities are. Well, what if I did nine and left my hardest and most valuable item? That might equate to around 60 percent of my potential productivity, even though nine items were crossed off my list. Well, what if I did the two most valuable tasks and two easier things? I'm over 90 percent for the day, even though I left six things on my list!

This is what's hard about productivity versus time management. Could you be more productive if you did four things instead of nine? Sure, if one or two of those tasks were among the "vital few," as Pareto called them. If you get the two big tasks done and then two more—and leave six items still on your list at day's end, knowing you completed the most critical items—how do you feel now? Doesn't it feel much better to get something valuable off your plate? Doesn't it make the rest of your day good? It's not about the number of things you check off your list; it's about *what* you're checking off.

The Two Pains

You have to identify the most essential tasks from the beginning by asking yourself, "What are my critical items? What have I been avoiding?" Those are the 20 percent of your activities providing 80 percent of your value. Are they easy? Are they fun? Do they make you think, "Yeah, I can't wait to get to work and do this"?

Probably not. They require a lot of concentration and aren't likely to be very enjoyable. Humans are wired to avoid pain. We would much rather do something pleasant, and this is something you're going to battle every day. Although pain in your business life is unavoidable, some of it is productive pain that makes you stronger in the long run and sets you up for success.

The late Jim Rohn always said you have the choice between two pains. The first is the pain of discipline. It's never easy to force yourself to do the difficult things. In every situation, we would much rather do the fun thing. It's painful to do what you know you need to do, especially when you don't feel like it.

But the only other option is the pain of regret: Looking back and realizing what you've missed because you didn't try hard enough. I would much rather tolerate the pain of discipline, because what I *don't* want is the pain of regret when I get to the end of the day and discover I didn't work my day the way I should have. I've either bought myself a late night, and now I can't get home and play with my kids, or I walk out banging my head on the wall because I'm so stressed out. I'm sure you feel the same way.

Yes, it's hard to stimulate the momentum you need when you're starting on a tough project or other task. It takes a lot of cracking the whip to overcome the procrastination. Remember when you were in school, and your professor assigned you a term paper in March that was due in May? When did you do the paper? If you're like most people, you did it in May, probably the night before it was due. How was your stress level in March? Fairly low. You told yourself, "I have two whole months to get this done!" But you procrastinate, and suddenly it's May, your stress level is sky-high, and you do it the night before. Maybe you have seven classes with similar papers due. The quality of your work is reduced, and your stress level has increased.

Keys to Productivity

You can decrease your stress level and avoid the pain of regret by using just three simple tools. Now, the practice isn't necessarily easy, but the tools themselves are simple. Cracking the whip of discipline is ultimately a lot less painful than regretting it all later.

1. *Focus*. Start working on the hard stuff *right now*, not later. Spend some time determining how to finish a difficult task given the deadline you have. You might find you have to write an average of 500 words a day on that big report to complete it before it's due; train yourself to write at least that much—if not more—every day. If you can exceed the limits you've set, you'll end up with a time cushion you can use to edit and polish the report until it shines. Don't let your emotions compel you to do the easiest things on your list just to get a little jolt of accomplishment. Emotions are bad judges about what's important and what you should be doing.

2. *Take care of yourself*. Few things waste as much time as feeling poorly. You need to shine physically, emotionally, and spiritually to do your best work. Otherwise, your mind wanders, you lose your focus, you feel so poorly you can't do anything, and your ability to take care of others decreases as well. If you're emotionally or spiritually off the rails, figure out where you got out of alignment with your values. Does your time reflect the things in life that are truly important to you? Keep asking yourself questions: "What's bothering me?" "What's happening in my life I don't like?" "What am I tolerating?" Figure out what you don't need to do in your life—whether it's watching excessive TV, attending the PTA, not exercising, or drinking too much caffeine—and quit doing them.

3. *Eliminate time-wasting behavior*. Where are the worst time abuses in your life? For many of us, they include random Internet surfing, socializing, and personal phone calls. Although these aren't inherently bad, you shouldn't be doing them when you should be working. Consider this: Suppose there was a video camera above your desk? Shades of Big Brother, but what would you change if you *knew* someone was watching?

The third annual Salary.com 2007 "Wasting Time Survey" reported the average employee wastes 1.7 hours of a typical 8.5-hour workday—a decrease from the 2.09 hours wasted per day in 2005. The number one culprit of wasted time: Internet use, at 34.7 percent; followed by socializing with coworkers (20.3 percent); and conducting personal business (17.0 percent).

Over 63 percent of respondents admitted to wasting time at work. The 20- to 29-year-olds waste almost twice as much time (2.1 hours) as 40- to 49-year-olds (1.4 hours). Keep in mind this does *not* take into account how much work people are doing at home and on weekends. SuperCompetents often work from home. In my opinion, the surveyors might be asking the wrong questions.

It's interesting to note wasted time has declined 19 percent since the first survey in 2005. Yes, you can point to a growing economy and increases in productivity. But is it possible people are wasting less time because they want to get things done more quickly and get the heck out of Dodge? Are they deciding they're going to control their technology better, rather than letting it control them? Perhaps this is symptomatic of a backlash against corporations that seem happy to work people to death. Workers have had it with their personal lives suffering, and a rebellion is building. SuperCompetent employees will be in a much better position to call the shots on when, where, and how much they'll work. By reducing wasted time at the office, they can get the results they need in less time and get home to their lives. It's a win-win situation for employer and employee: good for revenue and good for morale.

What will the results in 2010 and beyond show? How low can we go? Well, we can't eliminate all wasted time. People aren't robots. All socializing isn't bad; some is necessary for building relationships and stronger teams. Let your employees get on the Internet at lunch and buy a birthday gift for a spouse. Who cares? They go home, log back in, and continue working anyway.

Employers will have to get hip pretty quickly to the way people are working if they want to keep the best and the brightest. Then again, maybe employees are wasting time because they're underpaid, or there are system problems or computer issues, or politics, or horrible meetings, or a lack of challenging work. I wonder what the results would be if we turned the tables and surveyed the management on how *they* slow their employees down and cause them to waste time.

Time Wasters to Watch Out For

Here are some time wasters to avoid. Often they're not such a big deal when looked at independently, but collectively, they can add up.

1. *Sitting bombs*. You've passed the magazine 20 times—you know, the one with a great article for your mom—and keep telling yourself, "I need to send the article." Do it now. Whenever possible, dispatch routine tasks immediately. If it takes less than three minutes, do it at the moment you remember it.

2. *Appointments*. Your friend repeatedly cancels lunch dates at the last minute. This drives you crazy, but you continue to put up with it. Next time, don't. If the person is important to you, explain how frustrated you are. If it's a vendor, don't reschedule. If this is the person's best behavior in the beginning of the relationship, the reliability is only going to get worse.

3. *Waiting time*. It makes you nuts to have to continually wait for your doctor, who is always late (we must go to the same doctor!). Instead, you decide you'll make good use of this time and now carry note cards and magazines in your tote. Or switch doctors.

4. *Forgetfulness*. At the end of the day, you had to rush out the door and leave a project half-done. You're always frustrated, because when you return and look at the page, you can't for the life of you remember what you were thinking or doing. Before quitting for the day, jot a few notes on a sticky pad about where you left off and what your next step is.

5. *Post-vacation slam*. You return from vacation and are so overwhelmed by your overflowing inboxes, you're more stressed out than before you left. Decide instead to return a day earlier, so you can get unpacked, do the laundry, and sort your mail.

When something's bothering you, do a bit of introspection to see what's going on and how you might approach it more efficiently or effectively next time. If you're in a rut and have grown accustomed to low productivity, change may not be comfortable. It may not be easy, but it might be for the best. Take an honest look at your life, determine what isn't working any longer, and change it.

Always Running, Always Running Behind

To the average worker, the terms *busy* and *productive* are synonymous. The true SuperCompetent knows they can be completely different. Yes, of course you can be busy and productive; all

SuperCompetents are, most of the time. At some level, you *have* to be busy to be productive. But just because you're busy doesn't mean you're productive.

Confused yet? It's easy to get bogged down in unproductive tasks that keep you running all day but that don't accomplish anything of substance. Some of us spend our days putting out brushfires, responding repeatedly to this-will-only-take-a-minute requests that never do, in fact, take only a minute. In the end, they gang up on you, and you end up working all day on things that won't earn you as much money as you might make flipping burgers, when you should be making profitable decisions.

Then there are those of us who willfully lose focus and decide it will be okay to play a quick game of Solitaire here, to check our checking account balance there, or e-mail our cousin in Tampa. All these are small things that don't take long, but they disrupt your concentration and make it difficult to recover the focus necessary to get the job done. If you can tame this tendency, you'll be surprised how much you can accomplish.

Finally, stop wasting time when you're forced to wait on someone *else* to do something. If you're in line at the bank, read the latest report from the CFO on your Kindle, or bone up on one of your professional journals. Take a second and send an e-mail to a coworker on your BlackBerry. Take care of one of those little tasks you've had on your to-do list for a week—or a month. Draft a note to remind yourself of an important task. Instead of letting these forced waits drain your limited time, take care of things now, so you can relax when you should be relaxing.

SUMMARY: ACCOUNTABILITY

Unless you live in a totalitarian state or are an indentured servant (and I doubt either of those conditions apply), then it's all down to you when it comes to productivity. Super-Competent people accept both blame and credit when they're due. Distracted? Bored? Stymied by stupid procedures? Don't just sit there and fret. Don't whine and wish someone would do something. *You* do something. Get off your butt! Fix things. Question processes, strive continuously to improve yourself and the situation you're in, and practice self-discipline in all things. Focus on your work. Sit down, block out all distractions, and get to work with a will.

You also need to become comfortable making decisions without becoming paralyzed by any potential negative consequences. *Just do it.* Ultimately, this key boils down to accepting responsibility for yourself and what you need to improve. At this level, at least, *you* are the boss of you.

Go to www.TheProductivityPro.com/Accountability to receive bonus material, the SuperCompetent Key 5 assessment questions, a summary, and the action-planning worksheet in Microsoft Word format. Get additional resources, audios, videos, and more at www.SuperCompetentBook.com.

ACTION PLANNING WORKSHEET: ACCOUNTABILITY

21. I take personal responsibility for handling my time and productivity; I never lay the blame on anyone else.

    What came to mind when I read this?

    _____
    _____
    _____
    _____

    What is my action plan for improvement?

    _____
    _____
    _____
    _____

22. When I see an unusually lengthy and inefficient process, I do what I can to make it easier for everyone.

    What came to mind when I read this?

    _____
    _____
    _____
    _____

    What is my action plan for improvement?

    _____
    _____
    _____
    _____

23. Rather than waste even small amounts of time, I get right to work.

    What came to mind when I read this?

    _____

    _____

    _____

    _____

    What is my action plan for improvement?

    _____

    _____

    _____

    _____

24. When I have all the information I need to proceed, I make decisions quickly.

    What came to mind when I read this?

    _____

    _____

    _____

    _____

    What is my action plan for improvement?

    _____

    _____

    _____

    _____

25. I understand the difference between being busy and being productive: results.

    What came to mind when I read this?

    _____

    _____

    _____

    _____

    What is my action plan for improvement?

    _____

    _____

    _____

    _____

PART 6

SuperCompetent
Key 6: Attitude

SuperCompetent people always make an effort and practice positive thinking.

ATTITUDE is your motivation, drive, and proactiveness.

This key makes things happen with a can-do, winning outlook.

Your attitude is your state of mind and the way you perceive the world about you. Bill Schweber, Executive Editor at EDN.com, once wrote an article in which he described the difference between the founders of technology companies and the people hired to run them. The passion he describes is important. To sum it up, the high-powered gunslingers are fanatical about getting immediate results in their publicly traded enterprises, whereas the founders greatly want to influence the enterprise's future with the technology they create. The former take the short-term view; the latter have the long term in mind.

Of course, both short-term goals and long-term vision are essential to organizational success—both significantly drive accomplishment. Regardless of their roles, their attitudes exude the passion that commits fully to a course of action and sees it all the way through. The gunslingers' approach may mean finishing strong on a three-month project, whereas the founders' goals may require that they hit a 10-year profit target. Regardless of the method, their perseverance mind-set remains unchanged, which boosts fulfillment in their daily lives. Without this perspective, it's hard to continually put forth the effort needed to get a job done over a sustained period of time.

Maria Hannon, the Director of Human Resources at the Denver Museum of Nature and Science, told me, "The most successful people are those with the magical combination of personality and integrity you can feel. As I look at promotions, I want those who have been consistently driven, consistently innovating, and consistently flexible." Let's discuss how to be that person.

CHAPTER 26

If You Stew in Your Own Juices, You'll End Up Overcooked

SUPERCOMPETENT Hero Thinking:	I keep an eye on my stress level, realizing it would be a mistake to ignore my emotional health.
SIMPLY COMPETENT Zero Thinking:	If things don't let up, I'm gonna have a nervous breakdown—but I just don't have the time to slack off right now!

It's critical for you to pay attention to how you feel about your work environment and manage your mental health carefully. Emotions, stress, worry, and your temper can all conspire to bring you down, especially if you don't take the occasional break to recharge your batteries. When you ignore your need for rest, that need starts to boil over with worry, and the stress of worry leads to anger. If you've ever allowed yourself to get to the point of extreme stress—where you feel like there's a live wire inside you all the time—then you know how hard it is to maintain your temper, keep yourself from blaming others, and avoid being brusque, pessimistic, and easily annoyed. It might not be a problem if you were the only one affected. But you're not.

A dramatic example of how anger can affect others came in 1972, when an airplane crashed at Heathrow Airport in London. The postcrash investigation revealed that the pilot had been unhappy because of the way in which an airline strike had been settled. As he took the plane off the ground, he felt it to be badly off trim: The men who had loaded the cargo had carelessly failed to keep the weight in balance. The pilot, already angry, became furious and overcorrected by jamming his controls. The plane dived into the runway, and 118 men, women, and children were killed.

With any luck, your stress won't *literally* kill anyone. But it *can* kill team spirit pretty quickly. Snapping at people who are trying to help you is no way to encourage them to help you next time. Those negative emotions divide you from others and make you feel like you're isolated and dealing with your stresses on your own. Chances are you'd have lots of support if you'd take advantage of the assistance that others offer. This kind of attitude makes you no fun at parties and is bad for your health. This saps your energy, increases stress, etcetera, etcetera, and so forth—in a vicious cycle that becomes increasingly harder to break.

In addition to killing your social life, being irritated can actually kill you, too. In a 1987 study, psychiatrists at Duke University concluded people who have continuing feelings of hostility toward others have an increased risk of illness and early death. After examining 30 years' worth of data, they discovered those who scored high on questions measuring hostility were more likely to have died than those who scored low. People who scored in the top fifth for hostility had *four times* the death rate of people who scored in the bottom fifth.

Clearly, death is unproductive.

Dr. John Barefoot, who headed the study, told a meeting of the American Psychosomatic Society it's not known why this happens or if people can change their behavior. But he said, "It's not going to hurt people to adopt a more positive view of others."

Anxiety, worry, annoyance, and anger are contagious. You dumped on your secretary, you glared at the clerk, or you gave your coworker in the next office a tongue-lashing. Reactions like these increase others' stress levels, and then they pass it on. You might even get caught up in a never-ending cycle of negativity where you go home and snap at your wife, who yells at the kids, who kick the dog, which now needs to go to the vet. You snap at the vet, who was going to knock $30 off your bill, but now she doesn't—and you hate her. *Wow.*

Get a Grip

The first thing to do is to acknowledge the negative feelings a lack of control can create. You *do* have control over your friends, your love relationships, and your career. You decide for yourself what's right and what's wrong, whether you should stay in this weekend or go out, and whether to vote Democrat or Republican. You decide who to see, what to wear, and what to eat.

However, you have little effect on the government, economic policy, the rise and fall of the stock market, Mother Nature, international events, and even your company's overall direction. Changes can often disrupt your life and force you to shift your plans. There's usually little you can do, but you're dramatically affected by it. Accepting this means realizing you can't control certain things and should stop trying. You can sit around and wonder, "Oh my gosh, how is this going to affect me? What if I'm next to go? How will I pay the bills? I'm going to be a bag lady!" You stew, worry, and make yourself sick.

These things are going to happen. They just will. You'll get no warning, which can be frustrating. People will tell you to "reach for the stars—you can achieve whatever you want!" but they neglect to mention you might get hit by a comet in the process.

Like the old 12-step mantra says, it's time to accept the things you can't change and focus on the things you can.

Give Yourself a Break from the World

Try to stay positive, despite the doom and gloom. Overdosing on pessimistic, excessively dramatic news coverage is just going to weigh you down with bad thoughts—not good for those looking to clear their heads and get things done! It's important to be informed about what's happening in the world, but you definitely don't want to overdo it. Some business pundits will tell you to avoid the news altogether if you can. Although I wouldn't go that far, I do see their point.

For a while now, we've been bombarded with dismal economic news every time we turn on the television or pick up a newspaper. No wonder everybody seems to be in a rut. Follow the daily news to stay in the loop and understand the issues affecting your industry. After that, it might be time to shut off the TV and catch up on some fun reading—or, better yet, to spend some more time with family.

Don't Worry, Be Happy

Worry is a habit, so develop an awareness of it and monitor yourself. When you catch yourself worrying, replace the bad images with the best-case scenario. Have you ever thought, "Omigod, if I don't get this work done by Wednesday, I'll miss the deadline. If I miss the deadline, I'll lose the client, if I lose the client I won't get paid. If I don't get paid, I'll lose my house and my health insurance, and I'll be out on a street corner, living in a box, and dying of malnutrition."

You just created a worry within a worry within a worry. Think instead, "The client will be so pleased when he sees the work I've done." Be a talented optimist: "I'll get much more work from this client, and the regular assignments will raise my standard of living, and maybe I can buy the boat I've been eyeing!" Or better yet, you'll have free time to spend on your new invention (the flying car, of course).

Many people are such talented worriers they *worry about not worrying*. They're afraid if they stop worrying, they'll suddenly stop working, because they won't be motivated to action. I would argue the boat you've been eyeing is as good an incentive as living in a cardboard box at the side of the road is a *dis*incentive. Picture waxing up your new boat to feel the relaxing, positive emotions that allow you to be your most creative and open to your client. This kind of thinking will make your success much more likely than filling yourself with the anxiety you feel when you imagine yourself teetering on the brink of homelessness.

Dr. Charles Mayo of the Mayo Clinic has said: "Worry affects the circulation, the heart, the glands, the whole nervous system, and profoundly affects health. I have never known a man who died from overwork, but many who died from doubt." When you worry too much, when you isolate yourself from others, when your focus is only on your problems, you can't focus on your dreams.

What Do You *Mean* I'm Not In Charge of the World?

Sadly, you can't control everything in your life. You might have every moment scheduled to a fare-thee-well, but the moment you actually get out there and interact with the world, something's going to give.

Can you get the jerk ahead of you to quit driving 30 in a 45 mph zone? My husband will keep trying, but you probably won't, or at least not easily or sanely. If you're traveling via train from one city to another and a freight train derails across the track ahead, putting you hours behind schedule, what can you do? Nothing much. If a thunderstorm rains out the company picnic, you just have to deal with it. You're only human.

Be willing to accept that you simply do not have control over many things in life. Stop and get some perspective on the matter; five years from now, will it matter if you were a little late because of an unexpected traffic jam? What about five days or even five hours from now? Take it easy, stop worrying, and don't burn a hole in your stomach because you're stewing about things you can't change.

CHAPTER 27

Never, Ever, Ever, Ever, Ever, Ever, *Ever* Give In

SUPERCOMPETENT Hero Thinking:	Even when a task is monumental, I keep working at it until I whittle it down to size.
SIMPLY COMPETENT Zero Thinking:	Good grief! How am I ever going to get this done?

According to legend, Winston Churchill presented a speech in 1941 to a class at Harrow School that consisted entirely of the quote that I've used above as my chapter title—whereupon he sat down, completely finished. Sadly, it's a myth—the speech was over four minutes long—but his message, and the spirit behind it, are clear. Wise man. Whatever you want to call it—drive, effort, motivation, perseverance, tenacity, creativity—sticking to a task like glue until you're done is an important component of success in *any* endeavor. The same is true, perhaps even more so, for your goals and dreams. As the old Chinese saying goes, even a journey of a thousand miles begins with but a single step.

People who are positive, work hard, care about other people, and continually educate themselves will be more valuable to any organization. It's uncanny to me how many employers hire the wrong people and then wonder why their goals or businesses fail. You would think, since we've become a service-oriented society, that hiring managers would be concerned with hiring positive people—those who care about others are the ones who smile and have a kind word to say. Customer service is a vital element of any organization. When you hire a person who has all these attributes, your company will be better as a result of the positive person's efforts. These people are usually great at motivating others to get things done. They're good role models; they see the big picture.

When something seems impossible to do, you often don't even try, or you do it half-heartedly. Then, when it doesn't work, you say, "See, I told you I couldn't do it. It's impossible! I knew it was!" This is the famous self-fulfilling prophecy. If you think you can get better and be more productive, you can, and you *will*.

Always ask yourself, "What if?" Take stock. Consider your daily tasks and ask some important questions. "How can I do this better next time? How can I be more efficient? How can I get these results with less effort?" You can't just keep plowing ahead without occasionally regrouping and reassessing what you're doing—or what you have become blind to doing.

The Qualities of Perseverance

SuperCompetent people strive for the following six things:

1. *Inspiration.* Inspiration is all about flinging open the doors of your mind and letting new ideas wander inside. So stretch your mental horizons! Constantly learn and remain open to new sights, sounds, philosophies, and aesthetics. It might seem strange, but inspiration takes effort. It takes effort to visit a museum and be open to new ideas. It takes effort to study art, architecture, or theatre. But doing these things—gaining new inputs—will produce an inspirational wellspring from which you can continually draw.

   Making an effort at being inspired will also enable you to complete tasks in ways you never thought possible. By applying knowledge from other fields or activities to new projects, you're able to conceptualize solutions in new ways. Mastering the art of ideational inspiration will pay dividends well into your future.

2. *Motivation.* If inspiration is your well of creativity, motivation is the crank and bucket that allow you to dip into the well to achieve refreshing results. All the inspiration in the world won't accomplish anything if you don't muster the motivational energy to execute it. Ask yourself: What inspires you and keeps you working diligently all day? What drives you to move from inspiration to action? Identify your source(s) of motivation. When you get goose bumps or the hair on your forearms stands up with excitement, you can push through the extra mile, even in the face of tedious or unpleasant tasks. Remember: Your inspirational wellspring may well runneth over, but *motivation* is the key to harnessing the energy necessary to tap into your reservoir of ideas.

3. *Brass.* Being bold can take you far. For example: There was a brassy bathroom attendant working when I attended a showing of the play *Wicked* in New York City. Her pay was based on tips—so during the brief breaks during intermission, she made sure she was out there directing traffic, calling out when the next stall was available, encouraging people to hustle in order to get everyone through in the little time we had. She was also right there to hand people paper towels after they washed their hands. She was loud and fun and got lots of tips. It can't hurt to emulate her and hustle people (especially yourself) along, as long as you do it politely and with purpose.

4. *Effort.* Before my grandmother passed away in March 2009, she lived in a nursing home during the last years of her life. Like most nursing homes I've visited, it had an automatic coffee machine. You know—the kind where you punch a few buttons, tell it what flavor of coffee you want, what you want in it, and it shoots the cup down the little chute and makes your coffee for you. The first time I used this machine, there was a guy in front of me in line, so I thought, "Oh good, I can watch someone else do it first."

The guy took out a buck and tried to feed the machine, but the dollar was wrinkled and the machine wouldn't take it. So I handed him my dollar and said, "Here, try this one," and it worked. I watched him punch hazelnut, creamer, and sugar.

He stood back to watch it being made. The only problem was this machine trusted you would see the Styrofoam cups over on the counter; in this case, a cup didn't come down the little chute. Before either of us could react, the hazelnut coffee, creamer, and sugar went down the drain. I swallowed a loud guffaw. The man blinked, turned to me, and said, "Wow, this automatic stuff is efficient—it even drinks it for you. Gotta dollar?" "No," I said, trying not to laugh, "just this wrinkled one, and the machine won't take it."

Many people go through life hoping the machine will automatically drink it for them, and they won't have to work. Stop expecting things to just happen without action. You have to WORK. Put your nose to the grindstone and make your own coffee; grab a cup and roll up your sleeves!

5. *Urgency.* In his book *A Sense of Urgency*, John Kotter points out, "The opposite of urgency is not only complacency. It's also a false or misguided sense of urgency that is as prevalent today as complacency itself, and even more insidious."

    An old military adage says, "When uncertain, when in doubt, run in circles, scream and shout," which is a good example of false urgency. Sadly, it's a standard response to the unexpected in many organizations. They seem to think running around and staying busy are more important than actually getting things done. Being busy is fine—but if it's based on frustration or worry and doesn't accomplish anything, it's useless.

    True urgency is more a matter of perseverance and a tenacious personality than raw, unharnessed emotion. It might not mean you feel calm as such, but it's usually characterized by quiet competence rather than frantic activity, which only generates a lot of misdirected light and noise. It's energy, all right, but more like the wasted energy of a firecracker than the contained energy of an internal combustion engine. Sure, they're both an explosion; but the explosion inside the engine drives productive work.

6. *Going Above and Beyond.* Productive people tend to go above and beyond the call of duty, especially when they're *not* asked to do so. If your workload is a bit slacker than you like, you can point out to your manager where you're capable of taking on

more work or a favorite project. Don't overburden yourself, but if your manager is always working on activities that aren't of high value with pressing deadlines, point out that you're capable of making those decisions. If your manager complains that something is a waste of time, suggest that it be delegated to you. Consider asking for the following types of work:

- Decisions made frequently and repetitively
- Assignments adding variety to routine work
- Functions your manager dislikes or those with low value
- Work that will provide a new experience for you
- Tasks you know you're capable of handling
- Activities that will make you a more well-rounded employee and provide cross-training
- Opportunities to use and reinforce your creative talents
- Recurring matters involving minor decisions or time-consuming details

Practice Does Make Perfect

We hear over and over that the most important component of any endeavor is talent. Really? What about the talented hare that lost the race to the tortoise? Instead of applying himself, he fiddled around—and let the poky but determined turtle cross the finish line before the hare even got started. In his book *Talent Is Overrated: What Separates World-Class Performers from Everyone Else,* Geoff Colvin points out that while talent is indeed important, persistence and hard work can trump it. In other words, those who practice constantly are the ones who stand out. This echoes Malcolm Gladwell's 10,000-hour rule: By the time you've spent 10,000 hours doing anything, you've more or less become an expert, and the task comes naturally to you.

The Basics. A firm foundation of support and guidance can contribute heavily toward success—again, often more so than talent. Here's a fascinating example. Educational psychologist Benjamin S. Bloom once directed a study of 120 top young talents in fields as wide-ranging as mathematics, science, sports, and the arts. Despite diverse backgrounds, he discovered these successful young people had similar home environments while growing up: Their families were child-oriented, and their

parents did everything they could to help their children succeed. At the same time, however, a strong work ethic was evi-
dent. The children were encouraged to strive toward their goals,
meet their obligations, spend their time constructively, and
always put work before play. As Colvin put it, "In an organization, this would be called the culture—the norms and expectations that are simply in the air."

The Music Model. Direct and constant practice often leaves raw
talent in the dust. Do you think even the most talented musician
can pick up a guitar for the first time and play "In a Gadda Da
Vida" all the way through error-free? Not likely. Even if he's a mu-
sical savant, the sound will be off because he hasn't developed the
fingertip calluses necessary to coax the purest tones from the guitar. But given time and a thorough knowledge of the music—and,
of course, those all-important calluses—a dedicated musician will
edge increasingly closer to perfection.

The same applies to any business task, whether it's making presentations to coworkers or refining a manufacturing process. Yes,
it will start to get old over time, as you repeat it for the tenth or
hundredth or thousandth time—but repeat it you must. To avoid
the contempt of familiarity, remain conscious of each aspect of
the process and continually ask how it can be improved.

Eventually, it's good enough; indeed, by then, it may be wonderful. You'll never get there if you don't keep running through
the task over and over. As the tourist in New York was reportedly
told when he asked how to get to Carnegie Hall: "Practice, practice, practice!"

The Lowdown. There's a purpose to effective practice and consistent, thoughtful repetition, whether in the conservatory or in
your workplace: It's intended to improve performance. Like Con-
junction Junction in the old Schoolhouse Rock song, it'll get you
there if you're careful. Because, remember, talent isn't enough! To
get good at something, you have to do it over and over.

Many people are convinced you must ooze with talent to be
productive, which is a dangerous oversimplification of reality. Yes,
talent is always important—but talent without discipline is useless.
Potential untapped might as well not even exist, because eventually
it's going to dissipate without accomplishing anything. Ironically,
talent is one resource that grows when it's used. Lots of talented

children with potential fail, because they aren't encouraged or forced to do homework.

You need to practice, practice, and practice some more if you want to maximize whatever talent you have. Tenacity and a willingness to work are much more important than mere talent. Add support from friends and family, along with a strict adherence to obligations and goals, and you'll end up a SuperCompetent who'll dazzle the rest of us.

When the Going Gets Tough . . .

Woody Allen once said, "90 percent of success is just showing up"—and he's got a good point there. Consistently showing up is important, and then be willing to bull ahead no matter how difficult things look at first glance. I'm not talking about being naïvely optimistic, but realizing that if you're willing to put in some hard work and continue to do so—and practice what you're doing consistently—then even the largest task can be whittled down to something manageable. As the old Italian saying goes, "Everything is difficult before it becomes easy." This seems like a simple statement, almost a tautology, but there's a lot of wisdom there if you look closely.

This is especially important to remember when you're new at something. Remember when you first started driving? You sat with your eyes locked on the road and your mirrors, hunched over the wheel, hands precisely at ten and two. You demanded silence because you needed to concentrate; driving was a hard job. Five years down the road (so to speak), you're singing along with the radio, chatting with friends, and driving with one hand. This once-monumental task can now be accomplished without much effort.

At first glance, this may not seem to apply directly to difficult work projects, which are often of a singular nature, but it does. Once you've learned you can handle one, you realize you can handle others. This gives you the confidence to become an asset to the company, because you can take on anything and wrestle it down to size, or at least make a serious go of it. All you need to do is throw open your creativity and become inspired to tackle it, motivate yourself to do so, put in the necessary effort, and maintain the proper urgency to see it through.

CHAPTER 28

Monkey See, Monkey Do

SUPERCOMPETENT Hero Thinking:	I am creative and open to change; I always seek better solutions.
SIMPLY COMPETENT Zero Thinking:	We've always done things this way, so there's got to be a good reason for it. Who am I to try to make a change?

Start with a cage containing five apes. Hang a banana on a string and put stairs under it. Before long, an ape will wander over to the stairs and climb toward the banana. As soon as he touches the stairs, spray *all* the apes with cold water. The ape will quickly climb down. After a while, another ape will make an attempt with the same result: *All* the apes are sprayed with cold water. Continue until another ape tries to climb the stairs. Eventually, the other apes will prevent their buddies from climbing the stairs, seemingly the cause of the water.

Now turn off the cold water. Remove one ape from the cage and replace it with a new one. The new ape sees the banana and wants to climb the stairs. To his horror, all the other apes attack him! After another attempt and another attack, he knows if he tries to climb the stairs, he'll be assaulted. Next, remove another of the original five apes and replace it with a new one. The newcomer goes to the stairs and is attacked. The previous newcomer

215

takes part in the punishment with enthusiasm. Again, replace a third original with a new one. The new one makes it to the stairs and is attacked as well. Two of the four ape bullies have no idea why they weren't permitted to climb the stairs or why they're participating in the beating of the newest ape. After replacing the fourth and fifth original apes, all the apes that were originally sprayed with cold water had been replaced. Nevertheless, no ape ever again approaches the stairs. Why not? "That's the way we have always done it around here." (It often doesn't make any sense.)

Unleash Your Creativity

Why do we do things that don't make any sense, just because "we've always done it that way"? Let's give productivity another name: *creativity*. People tend to think of creativity as synonymous with imagination. They use it this way when they look at a statue of a lobster on top of a plastic phone at a modern art museum. "That's very . . . creative."

But this is not entirely true. The essence of creativity is *creation*. To be a creative person—to transform dreams into reality, to achieve greatness of any kind—you must create and you must produce. For this, you need your full energy. President Harry S. Truman once observed: "I studied the lives of great men and famous women, and I found the men and women who got to the top were those who did the jobs they had in hand, with everything they had of energy and enthusiasm."

Without the life force of productivity, there is no progress, no change, no experimentation, and no innovation. Businesses close early, and then don't open at all. Great goals are discarded, and then the little goals follow. Life becomes stagnant. But add the magic ingredient—the energy to produce and be creative—and doors fly open. New possibilities, opportunities, and worlds are opened to you.

Your productive energy is a critical element you can bring to your work, family, and life. It is the power to create, produce, and innovate. It may be the single most important ingredient that makes life's dreams possible. You can be an architect of the future.

Cheryl Roshak, President at Cheryl Roshak Associates, told me in a LinkedIn message: ". . . beyond all those attributes is tenacity, flexibility, and most importantly—creativity. Let me explain. Some people just never give up. They keep on going when others stop or say there is nothing that can be done. Those exceptional people are flexible; they can change course, or they can change fields or jobs either temporarily or permanently. Maybe go back to school for some training, take a step down to take a step up. They are more concerned with opportunity than with job titles, and sometimes even salary. And they live and think creatively. They approach situations with fresh ideas and present themselves confidently and creatively. There is always enthusiasm with a creative person, for they see possibilities where others don't. They tend to be doers and leaders, not followers, so people are naturally attracted to them. This doesn't mean they're smarter or better than other people—they are just different. They exude energy and confidence and are go-getters, not passive people, in my experience. They are survivors."

Refuse to Accept the Status Quo

Don't be afraid to think outside the box when it comes to getting things done. Use your imagination, even when you're tackling the most ordinary tasks. For example: If you're fed up with fighting your way through morning traffic, consider heading to work an hour earlier. Not only will you beat the rush, but you can use the extra time to get a jump start on work while the office is quiet, or just enjoy a cup of coffee at your desk while you catch up on some reading. Then you can leave an hour earlier, too, beat the *afternoon* rush—and spend more time at home.

If you're sick of being the family taxi, try carpooling to get the kids where they need to be. Hate cutting the grass? Hire it out to a trustworthy teenager. For a few dollars you can cut your stress (and your grass!) and free up some time.

Whatever the task, before you fall into the same old pattern, consider some alternatives. There might be a better way of doing things. At they very least, give it a shot.

What needs to happen to meet this deadline? While you fixate on a looming due date, it's only getting closer. You have a big project coming up in three weeks? Think about what needs to happen to get it done. Be specific. Instead of obsessing over it, develop your timeline in advance, and then figure out what it's going to take to see it through. Things will fall into place. This will also help you juggle your impending project with your other responsibilities.

Take Calculated Risks

In the summer of 2009, my husband John and I took a trip to Israel with our church, Cherry Hills Community Church; our friends the Sanborns; and about 200 other people. A fellow traveler was Joe Coors, of Coors beer fame. I had several lovely conversations with him and asked him about SuperCompetent people in his life. When I asked, "How do SuperCompetent people act when they fail?" Joe told me, "This is a real differentiator. Ninety-nine percent of people don't want someone to move their cheese or disturb their comfort zone. Super-Competent people relish the challenge to get in the game—not sit on the bench. Fear of failure for these folks in minimal; they accept that it will happen. They learn from the experience and get better."

Fear of failure is one of the most common reasons people don't succeed: They don't even try. But rather than sit there like a lump and accept the world as it is, take a look around. If something works well as it is, fine. If not, attempt to change it. Can you make things better for yourself and your company just by trying something new? Sure, there's always a possibility you can fail, which is why the pundits tell us that all business is managed risk; there's no ironclad guarantee you'll succeed. If someone tells you there is, they're probably lying.

Poker players have a term they call *expected value*. The most experienced among them can look at a hand and the contents of a pot at any stage of the game and tell you whether it has a positive or negative expected value; and if it has a positive expected value, they bet accordingly. You can take a page from their playbook: Look at what you're thinking about changing, weigh all the factors, and if it has a positive expected value, then make your bet.

What will happen if you fail? Well, look at it this way: If the chances of success are good, and the consequences of failure are anything less than financial ruin, maiming, or death, then why not give it a try? It may be you'll end up with a flush and win a big pot. But even if someone beats you with a full house, you're not necessarily out of the game—as long as you weighed the risks and didn't bet the house.

Resistance to Change

Sadly, most people tend to accept the status quo, whether you're talking about a corporate culture or a national one. To do otherwise might cause them discomfort. How else can you explain Nazi Germany or apartheid-era South Africa? Certainly, a significant portion of the populace had been brainwashed to believe certain things, but not everyone was. For a long time, most people were simply too lazy or too afraid to stand up for what was right.

On the other hand, the 56 signers of the U.S. Declaration of Independence were willing to sacrifice their lives, their fortunes, and their sacred honor to change a system they believed was corrupt. Many of them did those things.

With few exceptions, a workplace is neither as complex nor as dangerous a venue for change as the national or international stage. If you think a process can be changed for the better, suggest an improvement. You don't need to be rude about it, but don't hesitate to question a particular procedure or unstated rule if you don't understand why it's done that way. You may find there's a simple, logical explanation, or you may find it's done that way because it's *always* been done that way. There's no other reason, and no one has ever thought about it. They may be open to change. If you can impact the change, do it yourself. If that doesn't work, try something else, and then keep trying.

CHAPTER 29

Why Can't You Just Read My Mind?

SUPERCOMPETENT Hero Thinking:	I adjust my approach with difficult work and time styles; I work well with all different personalities.
SIMPLY COMPETENT Zero Thinking:	Why should I have to explain myself to anyone? I know what I mean. Can't they understand plain English?

In a perfect world, everyone in your work environment would raise the energy of the whole room. Everyone would be sunny and encouraging, and there would be no gossip or office politics or rude people. I'm sure your workplace is just like that. Am I right? No?

Perhaps your office is more like this Peanuts comic strip: Lucy shouts at Linus, "You blockhead!" Linus shouts back, "What did you call me? A dumbbell?" Lucy then says, "No, I didn't say dumbbell. I said blockhead." Linus smiles and walks away saying more to himself than to Lucy, "Oh, I thought you said 'dumbbell.'"

Then Lucy props her chin in her hands, psychologist style, and says, "That's what causes so much trouble between people today. There's no real communication!"

I'm Okay, You're Okay?

If you don't have any trouble dealing with anyone in your office, or if you're never bothered by the personality quirks of a coworker or boss, then you're either the sole proprietor of a home office—or aliens have replaced all the humans in your workplace with robots.

The main thing here is to realize other people probably aren't going to change. You might be able to tactfully and constructively point out a particular disruptive behavior, and you might willingly get a change, but people's basic personalities are pretty consistent. So you have only two choices: Get angry about it, or find a way to deal with it without getting wound up yourself.

First, take a moment to consider whether *you* might be the problem. It's common for intelligent, high-functioning Super-Competents to become frustrated with others. It may seem it takes the other guy twice as long to do a task you find easy. Then he complains he has too much work. Well, if he could only get it done faster! It's hard to be an eagle when surrounded by a flock of turkeys, right?

This thinking will get you nowhere. It's better to remind yourself of the words of the humorist Will Rogers, who said, "We're all ignorant, only on different subjects." It's quite possible someone else is looking at your work and thinking the same thing about you! I've had to learn the hard way that I can't place the same demands I have of myself on everyone else. Not everyone thinks like a SuperCompetent. So don't waste your mental energy psychoanalyzing your coworkers and trying to figure out what happened in their childhoods that's made them the way they are. You're not Dr. Phil.

Instead, look inside yourself and see if you can improve your own responses. Are you impatient with people? Do you let this show on a regular basis, without concern about how people will react? Gauge your verbal and nonverbal responses to people. Even if you're the most productive person in your office and you know it—and especially if you're too cocky—let me tell you this: When it comes to production, the perceived slacker is *nothing* compared to the verbally abusive person who tries to beat everyone down with insults—especially if that person is the boss.

Dealing with Difficult Personalities

One of the great challenges in life—all life, not just at work—is trying to deal with personalities you find difficult. Doing so poorly is a real drain on everyone's energy.

Politeness and similar social constructs that allow us to interact with other people at anything more than the most basic level have a purpose: They lubricate social interaction. If they didn't exist and allow us to come together and share our brilliance, then we'd still be living in caves in tiny family groups and cowering from saber-toothed tigers and dire wolves. Our ability to be social and work together effectively has given us dominion over this planet. Sure, the system breaks down, but it works more than it doesn't.

Still, no one should have to work in a toxic environment. If someone constantly interrupts you, let the person speak until he or she has finished. Then, when it's your turn and the person interrupts, say, "Excuse me, I didn't interrupt you when you were speaking, and I would ask you to do the same for me." Don't let truly inappropriate behavior go unchallenged. You don't need to be confrontational about it; just say something like, "We should take a few minutes and come back to this discussion when we've both had time to calm down."

If these types of things happen repeatedly, and you find you're going home each day with your stomach in knots, it could be time for a change. If the environment is detrimental to your mental and physical health—and it doesn't seem as though it will ever change—then take your talents elsewhere. When your energy is stolen and your creativity and worth are insulted in this way, your productivity plummets.

The 12 Dysfunctional Productivity Personalities

Most of us depend on others at some point in our day. Our colleagues' individual work styles and attitudes can have a huge impact on our own ability to get things done. The following is a list of 12 dysfunctional personal productivity personalities. Hopefully this list will help you smile (rather than cringe) the next time a coworker's bad habits start to drive you up the wall. I've also included some thoughts on how to deal with each of these pesky personalities. In no particular order:

1. *Scrappers.* A scrapper's desk usually looks like a modern art exhibit, covered in bits of paper and sticky notes. They write important notes on whatever is close at hand, whether it's a fast food receipt or the back of an envelope (a scrapper's favorite).

   Handling the Scrapper: You can't make a scrapper adopt a comprehensive planning system or force all those little scraps into Outlook or a BlackBerry. What you *can* do is make sure the items pertaining to your work don't get lost in the shuffle. Send follow-up e-mails detailing key meeting takeaways, check in before important deadlines, and never fail to follow up on a delegated task.

2. *Pilers.* Pilers have a lot in common with scrappers, except that it's generally much more difficult to navigate your way through the piler's office. They keep everything and file nothing. There will be boxes on the floor and every inch of desk space will be occupied by stacks of paper, generally piled up to the point where an archeologist could use them to figure out what the piler has been working on for the last five years.

   Handling the Piler: The best thing you can do for the piler is simple: Don't add anything to the piles. Chances are that any document, book, or report you put in their hands is going to end up in a heap someplace, where it is probably as good as gone. Never hand your only hard copy over to a piler unless you are ready to kiss it goodbye. And set clear deadlines. Their idea of giving something a high priority is placing it on their (generally largest) immediate-attention stack. Don't ask them to do something right away; ask them to do it by Tuesday.

3. *Multitaskers.* Multitaskers always have a thousand things going on at once and generally take pride in it. They flit from task to task, getting many things started but few things completed. And they often appear frazzled, overwhelmed, and scattered.

   Handling the Multitasker: Always use caution when working with a multitasker. These people will rarely admit they don't have the capacity to take on another task and can easily become distracted by competing priorities. Always double-check with multitaskers directly to make sure they can and will do what is expected in an agreed-upon time frame.

4. *Interrupters.* "Gotta minute?" It's practically the interrupter's catch phrase. They will constantly show up at your desk, disrupt your day, and derail your train of thought. Their interruptions are sometimes trivial and sometimes relevant but almost always ill timed.

   Handling the Interrupter: You have to be honest on this one. If someone asks if you have a minute, don't be afraid to tell the person that you don't. The more cautiously you guard your own time, the more others will begin to think twice before needlessly asking for it. A polite response to an interruption is to say, no, you don't have any time right now but would be happy to meet later in the day if needed. Additionally, a simple "Do Not Disturb" sign can go a long way—as long as you don't abuse it.

5. *Procrastinators.* Some people seem clinically incapable of doing anything before the last possible moment. They start things with just enough time to squeeze them in before the deadline. You'll also notice procrastinators tend to put off high-value (often challenging) tasks in favor of more pleasant, less critical ones.

   Handling the Procrastinator: Don't let a procrastinator drag your project team down. The best way to get out ahead of him or her is to plan in advance and evaluate results on an ongoing basis, not just when the work is done. If your procrastinator is expected to deliver a weekly progress report, he or she will be more likely to stay on track. Of course, you should probably steer clear immediately before your meeting, which will be crunch time.

6. *Socializers.* Socializers waste inordinate amounts of time chatting with coworkers and keeping up with the personal lives of everyone at the office. They're great at planning the company party but tend to fall short in other ways.

   Handling the Socializer: Socializers do what they do because they get something out of it—interaction, stress relief, distraction from work, whatever. If you don't have anything along those lines to offer, they'll lose interest in you pretty quickly. You just need to be sure not to play along. If you're in the habit of nodding your head and smiling while others talk your ear off, then you are part of the problem. Politely state you need to get back to what you were doing to keep your day on track.

7. *Meeting Addicts.* Some people love to call meetings. Maybe they enjoy the setting and the interaction. Or maybe it has never occurred to them it's possible to get things done without putting half the department around a conference table. Either way, the result is a lot of time wasted by everyone involved.

   Handling the Meeting Addict: First of all, don't be afraid to decline a meeting when it's appropriate to do so. Explain you don't feel your presence is needed and ask to be kept in the loop on any important outcomes affecting your work. Second, don't be afraid to suggest an alternative to a meeting. When you get the request, simply call the organizer to ask if the matter could be handled by e-mail or conference call. In fact, you might be able to resolve the issue on the spot and save everyone a lot of time and disruption.

8. *Crisis Creators.* We've all been there. A lack of planning by one person leads to a crisis for everyone else. Even minor issues are exaggerated into a full-blown disaster, and everyone involved ends up feeling stressed and drained as a result. Crisis creators seem to always be fighting fires, and coworkers are often dragged into the fray.

   Handling the Crisis Creator: Unfortunately, we often have to step in and help fight fires even if they aren't our fault. If a certain individual is constantly working in crisis mode, it is important to not play into the drama. Keep a cool head and don't get stressed. Then, once the crisis is resolved, insist on a debriefing meeting to figure out what went wrong. Once crisis creators realize problems aren't going to be forgotten once the crisis is over, they'll be more inclined to stay out of trouble in the first place.

9. *E-mailers.* These people send e-mails for everything. It doesn't matter how simple or how complicated an issue is; an e-mail message is the answer for them. They never use the phone,

they never walk across the hall to deliver a 10-word message, and they usually LOVE the "Reply All" button.

Handling the E-Mailer: Usually you won't have much luck influencing the e-mail habits of a colleague. What you CAN do is set clear expectations concerning your own use of e-mail. Tell coworkers you can only check your messages a few times each day, so they don't expect you to treat Outlook like an instant messaging service. People are generally pragmatic about things, and if e-mail isn't a good way to get a response from you, they'll stop using it for everything.

10. *Packrats.* Packrats have never thrown anything away in their professional lives. They don't worry about the company's records-retention policy, because they retain everything, no matter what. They are often overwhelmed by their own treasure trove of obsolete documents—which will come in handy if you ever need to take a look at the final report from the cancelled project from 1986.

Handling the Packrat: Packrats are sometimes highly organized creatures, but they are often more worried about the thickness of their project files than they are about what's inside. Never trust a packrat to manage priorities or to take away the key points from any given interaction. Be direct about what you need from them, so you don't end up with a ton of unnecessary research or extraneous background information. Just the facts, please.

11. *Perfectionists.* By insisting on doing everything perfectly, perfectionists generally fail to accomplish anything at all. They work hard but complete little. Perfectionists keep meticulous meeting notes, promise the world during planning sessions, and often seem to crack up just as the project is coming together.

Handling the Perfectionist: When you are working with a perfectionist, it's a good idea to plan for frequent touch points throughout the project. Rather than expecting to reconvene at the end, schedule several synch-up meetings along the way. This will help keep the perfectionist working in manageable (if imperfect) chunks and also provide a chance to dazzle you with little presentations throughout the project. Perfectionists just love that!

12. *Workaholics*. The workaholic works an 80-hour week and never misses an opportunity to remind you of it. It's puzzling, however, because they seem to accomplish less than others who work half the hours. The workaholic typically has no boundaries between work and home life.

Handling the Workaholic: To a workaholic, *end of day* does not mean five o'clock. Usually, it means "before tomorrow." When you are expecting something from a workaholic, keep in mind you will likely see an e-mail roll in at 10:45 PM. Also remember that workaholics have no sense of urgency. Because they plan to be working into the evening anyway, they tend to waste time during normal business hours. You can subtlety nudge them in your direction by saying things such as, "I'd like to have this returned by three o'clock so I can be out the door on time tonight."

While a few of these 12 dysfunctional productivity personalities will bring some of your coworkers to mind, I hope you see that each of us has a little of one or more of these personalities in us as well. So as we work to deal better with our chronically troublesome coworkers, we should also be willing to improve on our own areas of personal dysfunction, which is a sign of a SuperCompetent!

Focusing on Teamwork

You can always make the argument, "But why should I care if my overall productivity drops because of other people's lack of civility? I'm not just a cog in the machine, after all. I'm not a robot. My value isn't measured by the sheer number of tasks I complete."

Although you don't have to take insults and mistreatment from anyone, you need to be able to fit into the organization or team of which you're a part with as few rough spots as possible. Here are some things you can do:

• Look for ways to help out your peers, subordinates, and superiors.

- Go out of your way to help others around you.
- Be team-oriented—a good follower as well as leader.
- Do your best to get along well with all types of people up and down the organization, regardless of position.

Play Nice

You can't control how people respond to you—but you can always control how you respond to *them*. Politeness and courtesy are the prime lubricants of social interaction. Some people aren't going to make an attempt to work with you no matter what you do, but you'll be surprised at how many people will, as long as you're nice to them. It may take effort, but it'll pay off in the long run. I'm not saying you should be a doormat and allow yourself to be taken advantage of in every situation, but you do need to be friendly, helpful, and willing to work as part of a team.

CHAPTER 30

Hello There, Pollyanna!

SUPERCOMPETENT Hero Thinking:	I am a positive person, even in negative circumstances.
SIMPLY COMPETENT Zero Thinking:	I don't give a darn what anybody thinks about me. If I feel gloomy, it's going to show, and everyone can deal with it.

Given the current economic environment, it's safe to say it's time we all got back to the basics and equipped ourselves with the abilities and attributes we need to work better and more responsibly. Some people seem to do this naturally. When unemployment strikes and people lose their jobs, SuperCompetents are the last ones standing.

It largely boils down to attitude. I'm not just talking about how SuperCompetent people view their jobs in general, but how they address their work, treat other people, handle change, and take the steps necessary to fix things when their best-laid schemes have blown up.

I've identified five attitude factors that separate the best workers from the crowd. Interestingly enough, these factors tend to be so intertwined they're difficult to separate into discrete categories. Here's what you have to do, in terms of adjusting your attitude, to be truly SuperCompetent.

1. *Adopt a Positive Approach to Your Work.* It may sound a tad clichéd, but in many work situations, an upbeat, can-do attitude does trump just about everything else. Businesses and other organizations love positive people, because they make social interaction so much more bearable. Now, I'm not saying an upbeat lazy worker is worth more than a dour productive worker, but a positive attitude does make up for a multitude of sins, and it's much easier to deal with than a dismal one. Plus, relentlessly positive workers are more likely to keep pushing forward when other people give up.

   Upbeat people also tend to work and play well with others, always a desirable trait in the business world. Their sense of teamwork is finely honed; they know two (or more) heads are usually better than one. Rather than being smug prima donnas, they're willing to subsume their own personalities as necessary. They're better able to connect with people and accommodate their flaws, and they are aware that they aren't perfect either. They've recognized an important truth: Teamwork is what helps people overcome their flaws by offsetting them with the skills possessed by others. After all, the whole point of diversity is finding an ability you lack—such as patience, artistic ability, or a mind for numbers—in someone else who has it in abundance. Diversity is one of Mother Nature's greatest ideas, and it's one reason human beings (and life in general) have mastered nearly every environment on the planet, and a few off it.

2. *View Adversity as Opportunity.* One reason the best workers manage to remain consistently optimistic is their tendency to reframe challenges, change, and adversity as opportunities. They don't just make lemonade when life hands them lemons; they make the rinds into zest and candy, too. They see *everything* as an opportunity, rather than being blinded by depression or paralyzed by indecision when something goes awry.

   Part of this tendency derives from their willingness to work hard and try new things; the saying "you can't teach an old dog new tricks" means nothing to the SuperCompetent. Let's be realistic here: The only reason the saying is *ever* true is because most people simply refuse to learn new things when the old ways no longer work. They'd much rather wallow in self-pity and force the universe to be the way they want it to be.

The problem here is that too many workers have a sense of entitlement. The world isn't set up to provide for you; if you think otherwise, your sense of entitlement is showing. *You* need to provide for yourself and those you care for—rather than, as Blanche Dubois would have it in *A Streetcar Named Desire*, "Depend on the kindness of strangers." (Look where that got her!). I truly believe the Lord does help those who help themselves. What the lazy call luck, the rest of us recognize as hard work and flexibility.

Productive people don't just stop working when they don't know how to do something; they learn how to do it and often spend their own time and money to do so. It's up to you to leverage your strengths and correspondingly shore up or complement your weaknesses. If you have to reinvent yourself to succeed as the business environment changes, do so. It may not be enjoyable, it may not even be fair—but it is *necessary*.

You're not a whiner or victim. You're a winner and victor, and you have to continue to think this way. Step up to the plate and knock a home run. If you have to buckle down and learn the basic rules of baseball first, and then exercise like mad to get into shape before you can hit a home run—then so be it!

3. *Demonstrate a Strong Work Ethic*. Here again, we see the value of good, steady work—and another example of why it's so difficult to dissect a valuable worker's attitude into individual categories.

    A willingness to put in the hours when and as necessary is the core of any strong work ethic, but there's more to it than that. A strong work ethic is supported by a framework of integrity, tenacity, and personal responsibility. You're value-driven, and you don't waste anyone's time. You're *never* late for anything that matters, like a job interview. You follow up consistently to make sure things get done (without being a micromanaging bother). You respect other people and their work, and you respect yourself and *your* work. You don't give up; you put your head down and push ahead, getting things done and done right.

4. *Maintain a Service-Oriented Attitude*. SuperCompetent people have realized something it takes others quite a while to get through their skulls: Whatever we do for a living, with few exceptions, *we're here to help others*. Even the job of the president

of the United States is to serve the people (although that was conveniently forgotten on a few occasions).

Good workers have passion for their jobs and the people they serve, whatever direction service may flow: up to their bosses, clients, and customers; down to subordinates; or laterally to coworkers. SuperCompetents have good communications skills, because they've worked to develop them. This is an important step toward creating mutually trusting, respectful relationships with the people they deal with regularly. And when it comes down to it, business is all about relationships. Who wants to make just a single sale to someone, when you can develop a long-term relationship with them and make many sales over the course of a lifetime?

A poor understanding of the value of customer service can be crippling in the business world. Here's a recent and particularly egregious example: Circuit City. Remember them? This example is doubly ironic, since Circuit City paved the way for other big-box electronics/appliance behemoths by proving they could succeed by offering good value and great customer service.

Back in mid-2007, Circuit City's board of directors decided they needed to cut costs—one of the standard methods of increasing profits. Alas, they didn't handle it well. For unclear reasons, the board decided the best way to cut costs was to lay off an entire category of workers and replace them with lower-paid newbies. The category chosen happened to be the senior sales reps, who were earning a princely \$12–\$14 per hour. Because there were thousands of people earning this rate who were replaced with folks earning just over minimum wage, this made for substantial savings indeed.

However, it wasn't long before Circuit City stock was trading at less than \$2 a share, down from a high of almost \$30— and the board was forced to pay out hefty retention bonuses to keep senior execs from flying the coop. Why was their stock tanking? Partly because the new sales reps didn't know their jobs well, and they couldn't help the hordes of people who were wondering how to set up their new smart phones and Xboxes, not to mention their LED and plasma screen TVs— especially in light of the new HDTV broadcast standard. People stopped going to Circuit City in droves. Why bother when you could get the same stuff for lower prices and at the same level of technical expertise at Wal-Mart? It became obvious far too late in the game that one of the reasons people had shopped at Circuit City was for the helpful, knowledgeable salespeople—the same ones the company had canned in their cost-saving measure. It was as if Circuit City had sewn its own mouth shut in order to save money on food.

If you haven't seen any Circuit City ads lately, it's because the company starved to death in early 2009. Admittedly, there were other things leading to the Circuit City's demise (it attributes its ultimate demise to the lack of consumer spending and overall economic downturn), but their cavalier attitude toward customer service was a significant factor. The Circuit City brand is now owned by Systemax, which uses the brand to sell electronics as an online retailer.

Customer service truly matters in *every level* of business. It never hurts to go the extra mile when serving others, especially in combination with other things I've described in this chapter.

5. *Be Willing to Attack Problems Head-On.* This facet of attitude flows naturally from a combination of the others. I've mentioned before that the best workers are willing to assess what they lack and seek to rectify it; they don't just sit there and mope. Nor do they let change—or the things other people would consider challenges or adversity—stop them for long. They reframe them as opportunity and keep on trucking.

Mix all this together with a good worker's optimism and fondness for teamwork, and what do you have? A creative problem solver. SuperCompetent people are flexible, strategic thinkers, and agents of change, who are willing to step forward and either fix things or advocate fixing the things they can't control. They're not after change for the sake of change; they want to make things easier for themselves and others. They're doing what most businesses ask of their employees but rarely actually value: thinking.

It's all part of accepting and embracing change, and it makes them stand out from the crowd, because they're not abrogating control over their work life, as so many people do when things become uncertain. They're not just grabbing something and holding on, either. They're molding the flux in their image.

Perky Is as Perky Does

There's attitude, and then there's *attitude*. Nobody likes dealing with a cocky smart aleck who wields what little power he or she has like a mugger wields a knife, much less a whiny wet blanket or a faceless drone who just does what he or she has to in order to get by. Those are the expendables—the people most likely to get the axe when times get tough. So you clearly don't want to fall into any of those categories.

A positive attitude makes up for a great deal. If you're ready and willing to be there and help everyone succeed, then when times get tough, your bosses will go out of their way to keep you on board (you don't have to suck up to them either; nobody much likes a toady). Just do your job, work with the team, be upbeat and attentive, and you're unlikely to have to worry about a pink slip. This applies whether you're a desk jockey, assembly line worker, middle manager, or a self-employed artisan who depends on building comfortable, mutually rewarding relationships with your individual clients in order to sustain your career.

SUMMARY: ATTITUDE

Kathy Goodin-Mitchell, Human Resource Director at Promotional Products Association International, told me, "I think two things make people stand out: (1) A willingness to go the extra mile, and (2) A vision for the future. If you have a person [with] these two [qualities], then you have an important person in your organization. These folks seem to have energy and ideas, enjoy their jobs, and are usually the ones you look to for the future. It's no longer good enough to just show up or do what is listed on the job description. I encourage my employees to think out of the box and look across the organization for their next steps or to learn more."

SuperCompetent people have these characteristics in common, and it's not as simple as having a so-called Type A personality or a willingness to work yourself to a frazzle. It's all about attitude and being willing to look beyond (or around or under) the expected.

Heaven knows it's easy to get down and depressed. It doesn't take long to realize life can be difficult, people can be annoying, and Lady Luck doesn't always roll your way. You shouldn't, however, give in to despair or irritation just because you can't control every little piece of your life or schedule. We mere mortals have to deal with reality once in a while.

In a similar vein, you shouldn't give up just because something looks hard. Take a look at the Taj Mahal or the Empire State Building—even the Pyramids of Giza or the Great Wall of China. They appear to be impossibly monumental structures, something humans couldn't possibly have created. But we *did*. Architects and builders, both ancient and modern, did it by focusing on tasks they were able to complete, one at a time, and then build upon: Lifting a marble slab into place, welding a steel beam, or quarrying a massive chunk of limestone without explosives (a difficult task indeed, but still doable). The lesson we can learn from them? Keep working at your project, recruit help if you need to, and you'll get it done.

Never meekly accept that the way things are done is necessarily the best way. Maybe it is, but you'll never know unless you evaluate how effectively it works, and how well it fits in with the rest of the process. Don't hesitate to propose a change if you think something else might work better. Your suggestion may not be accepted, and you may, in fact, come to believe the current method is best; but on the other hand, it might not have changed simply because of cultural inertia, and the way things have been done may no longer be the best way to do them.

It also makes sense to make every effort you can to communicate clearly and effectively with everyone you work with, and to learn how to handle even the most difficult personalities with skill and panache. You don't need to let people walk all over you, but you do need to be willing to accommodate different personalities, points of view, and the various emotions and circumstances affecting other people's behavior on a daily basis.

So be upbeat; be positive; and always have a can-do attitude about work and what you can accomplish. A particular task may seem outrageously difficult, and it may seem impossible for any human to accomplish it, but here's one thing I know for sure: If you don't try, you'll *definitely* never get it done. If you jump right in, show your willingness to be part of a team, and to make the proper effort to accomplish whatever needs to be done, you'll become insanely productive. Do this right, and you'll end up so far ahead, you'll wonder when you even passed the finish line.

Go to www.TheProductivityPro.com/Attitude to receive bonus material, the SuperCompetent Key 6 assessment questions, a summary, and the action-planning worksheet in Microsoft Word format. Get additional resources, audios, videos, and more at www.SuperCompetentBook.com.

ACTION PLANNING WORKSHEET:
ATTITUDE

26. I keep an eye on my stress level, realizing it would be a mistake to ignore my emotional health.
    What came to mind when I read this?

    _____

    _____

    _____

    _____

    What is my action plan for improvement?

    _____

    _____

    _____

    _____

27. Even when a task is monumental, I keep working at it until I whittle it down to size.
    What came to mind when I read this?

    _____

    _____

    _____

    _____

    What is my action plan for improvement?

    _____

    _____

    _____

    _____

28. I am creative and open to change; I always seek better solutions.

What came to mind when I read this?

_____

_____

_____

_____

What is my action plan for improvement?

_____

_____

_____

_____

29. I adjust my approach with difficult work and time styles; I work well with all different personalities.

What came to mind when I read this?

_____

_____

_____

_____

What is my action plan for improvement?

_____

_____

_____

_____

30. I am a positive person, even in negative circumstances.

What came to mind when I read this?

_____

_____

_____

_____

What is my action plan for improvement?

_____

_____

_____

_____

CONCLUSION

Why is becoming SuperCompetent so important? I can think of many reasons, starting with the natural desire so many of us possess to improve ourselves. But here's another: We're living during some pretty tough economic times. We've seen how some of the self-congratulatory leadership mantras of the last decade have resulted in unstable companies and an all-too-flimsy worship of glitz, glamour, and questionable management practices. Many of us suspected (even if we didn't say so) that sooner or later, we'd come to a place where the excitement would end and everyone would again get down to brass tacks—or else. Well, this is the place. Article after article lately has told us what we already knew: This is a time to get back to basics and equip ourselves with the abilities and attributes we'll need to live and work more responsibly and well.

One great reason to build up our competence is admittedly self-serving: We want to keep our jobs when those around us may be losing theirs. In recessionary times, with a faltering economy, with layoffs rampant and unemployment soaring, will you be the person left standing when all those around you fall? Master the six keys of the SuperCompetent person, and you'll have given yourself an insurance policy. And becoming SuperCompetent will serve you when the economy is strong again, too. In fact, learning the six keys will allow you to compete successfully in just about *anything* you try.

Being SuperCompetent, though, isn't just about surviving hard times or winning at the workplace. It's about mastery, and it has psychic rewards all its own. When you're on top of your game in one part of your life, you'll be on top of your game in all parts.

This I know for sure: There is no single road to this type of success. It doesn't work the same way for every person who tries it. Depending on personal characteristics, circumstances, and the resources available, different individuals will take their own personally tailored paths to success, maximizing their potential in ways startlingly unique and individualistic.

However, you'll never be successful (whatever success means to you) without learning to be productive. Yes, I'll admit there are occasional exceptions disproving the rule—Milli Vanilli, lottery winners, and certain heiresses who are famous for being famous come to mind. But those are flukes, of course; any reasonable person will realize achieving this type of success isn't likely to happen under ordinary circumstances. And even if it does happen, there's no promise it'll be more than temporary.

To be consistently successful, you need to be consistently productive, which requires you to put it all out there and to adhere to the concepts I've outlined in this book. For the sake of convenience, I've defined what I perceive as the top six productivity keys in this alliterative fashion: Activity, Availability, Attention, Accessibility, Accountability, and Attitude. You can call them what you want, but I'm convinced each and every one is crucial to achieving truly effective productivity in _any_ work environment—whether your boss is the same person who looks you in the mirror in the morning, or some anonymous executive deep in the bowels of a Fortune 500 company.

Each key requires close attention to and a profound understanding of your own strengths, weaknesses, and capabilities in all areas in order to truly excel. Although you need to focus on them individually, when they're implemented together as an effective productivity plan, you'll blossom into the SuperCompetent achiever who wows superiors and coworkers alike—and leaves the competition eating your dust.

Now that you've read this book (congratulations!), I recommend that you go back and read it again! Take notes, write in the margins, highlight specific sections with brightly colored markers, and place sticky tabs wherever you want to indicate the things you need to work on. This is a book you can turn to again and again for inspiration, as well as for useful ideas to help supercharge your SuperCompetence.

But remember this: No matter how many times you read this book, and no matter how many plans you make to jumpstart your productivity, you're never going to get anywhere until you get to work. Put these keys into Action (hey, another *A*).

If you bought a Ferrari, would you leave it in the garage where no one could see it? Not likely. Just as it makes no sense to purchase a top-flight high-precision machine and never use it, it's useless to make productivity plans you'll never put into action. Nobody's going to do it for you. There aren't any productivity elves in the basement who are going to spring into action at night and get your work done for you—no matter how much you might wish for it.

What another wise man named H.L. Mencken once said about success is so true: "The reason some people don't recognize opportunity when it knocks is because it comes in the form of hard work." You can't let the idea of hard work put you off. My hope for you is you take action today to cure any lack of productivity. My desire for you is to unleash the life you've always dreamed of—a life bursting with productivity and prosperity.

You can do it. And when you do, please send me an e-mail at Laura@TheProductivityPro.com, so I can celebrate with you in your SuperCompetent successes!

APPENDIX

Popular Productivity Blogs

Excerpted from ZenHabits.net.

43 Folders	www.43folders.com
Achieve IT!	www.persistenceunlimited.com
Black Belt Productivity	www.blackbeltproductivity.net/blog
Change your thoughts	www.stevenaitchison.co.uk/blog
Craig Harper—Motivational Speaker	http://craigharper.com.au
Daily PlanIt	http://dailyplanit.wordpress.com
David Seah	www.davidseah.com
Dumb Little Man	www.dumblittleman.com
Effective Time Management	http://timetricks.blogspot.com
Get Rich Slowly	www.getrichslowly.org/blog
Getting Finances Done	www.gettingfinancesdone.com
Getting Things Done	http://gtd.marvelz.com/blog
HD Biz Blog	http://hdbizblog.com/blog
Ian's Messy Desk	www.ismckenzie.com
Laura Stack—The Productivity Pro	www.theproductivitypro.com/blog
Leadership Training | Cultivate Greatness	www.cultivategreatness.com
Legal Andrew	www.legalandrew.com
Life Optimizer	www.lifeoptimizer.org
LifeClever	www.lifeclever.com

LifeDev	http://lifedev.net
Lifehack.org	www.lifehack.org
Lifehacker	http://lifehacker.com
Make It Great! with Phil Gerbyshak	http://makeitgreat.typepad.com
Managing with Aloha	www.managingwithaloha.com
Matt's Idea Blog	http://ideamatt.blogspot.com
My Empty Bucket	www.myemptybucket.com
Neat Living Blog	www.neatliving.net
Open Loops	http://hwebbjr.typepad.com/openloops
Passion Meets Purpose	www.passionmeetspurpose.com/blog
patrickrhone.com	http://patrickrhone.comjournal
Personal Development For A Greater Life	http://lifecoachesblog.com
Pick the Brain	www.pickthebrain.com/blog
Productivity Cafe	www.productivitycafe.com
Productivity501	www.productivity501.com
ProductivityGoal	www.productivitygoal.com
Scott H Young	www.scotthyoung.com/blog
Slacker Manager	www.slackermanager.com
Steve Pavlina	www.stevepavlina.com/blog
steve-olson.com	www.steve-olson.com
Success Begins Today	www.successbeginstoday.org/wordpress
The Cranking Widgets Blog	http://blog.crankingwidgets.com
The Daily Saint	www.thedailysaint.com
The Positivity Blog	www.positivityblog.com
The Simple Dollar	www.thesimpledollar.com
Web Worker Daily	www.webworkerdaily.com
Wise Bread Personal Finance Forum	www.wisebread.com
Your Life. Organized.	http://monicaricci.typepad.commonica_ricci_organizing_e
Zen Habits	http://zenhabits.net

INDEX

ABOUT THE AUTHOR

Laura Stack, MBA, CSP, is a personal productivity expert, author, and professional speaker, who is dedicated to building high-performance productivity cultures in organizations by creating Maximum Results in Minimum Time® with greater profits. She is the president of The Productivity Pro®, Inc., a time management training firm specializing in productivity improvement in high-stress organizations. Since 1992, Laura has presented keynotes and seminars on improving output, lowering stress, and saving time in today's workplaces. She is one of a handful of professional speakers whose business focuses solely on time management and productivity topics. Laura is a high-energy, high-content speaker, who educates, entertains, and motivates professionals to improve workplace productivity.

Laura is the bestselling author of four published books, including *The Exhaustion Cure* (Broadway Books, 2008), *Find More Time* (Broadway Books, 2006), and *Leave the Office Earlier* (Broadway Books, 2004), which was hailed as "the best of the bunch" by the *New York Times* and listed on the June 2004 Book Sense Business & Economics Bestseller list. *Leave the Office Earlier* has been published in seven countries and five foreign languages, including Japanese, Korean, Chinese, Taiwanese, and Italian. She is also a contributor to two of the popular *Chicken Soup for the Soul* books. Laura's popular monthly electronic newsletter has subscribers in 38 countries. She is a Certified Specialist in Microsoft® Office Outlook.

Widely regarded as one of the leading experts in the field of employee productivity and workplace issues, Laura has been featured nationally on the *CBS Early Show*, CNN, NPR,

Bloomberg, NBC TV, WB News, the *New York Times, USA Today*, the *Wall Street Journal, O Magazine, Forbes, Working Mother, Entrepreneur, Reader's Digest, Woman's Day*, and *Parents* magazines. Laura has been a spokesperson for Microsoft, 3M, and Office Depot, and she is the creator of The Productivity Pro® planner by Day-Timer. Her client list includes top Fortune 500 companies such as Starbucks, Wal-Mart, Microsoft, IBM, GM, MillerCoors, the Denver Broncos, Lockheed Martin, Time Warner, and VISA, plus a multitude of associations and governmental agencies.

Laura holds an MBA in Organizational Management (University of Colorado, 1991), integrating the importance of productivity in business with employee retention and satisfaction. She is the 2011–2012 president of the National Speakers Association (NSA) and is the recipient of the Certified Speaking Professional (CSP) designation, NSA's highest earned designation.

Laura lives with her husband and three children in Denver, Colorado.

For more information on hiring Laura to speak at your upcoming meeting or conference:

Laura Stack, MBA, CSP
President, The Productivity Pro®, Inc.
Laura@TheProductivityPro.com
www.TheProductivityPro.com
www.linkedin.com/in/laurastack
Phone: (303) 471-7401